The Turbocharged Company

Other Books by Larry Goddard

Corporate Intensive Care — Why Businesses Fail And How To
Make Them Succeed (York, 1993)

The Turbocharged Company

Igniting Your Business to Soar Ahead of the Competition

Larry Goddard and David Brown

YORK
PUBLISHING
COMPANY

Edited by Mark D. Kozel
Book Cover Design by Concialdi Design

For volume purchases and discounts, contact York Publishing Company at 216/491-0231 (phone), 216/491-0251 (fax) or Yorkpub@aol.com (e-mail).

Library of Congress Catalog Card Number 95-60619

Publisher's Cataloging in Publication

Goddard, Larry.
    The turbocharged company : igniting your business to soar ahead
  of the competition / Larry Goddard and David Brown.
    p. cm.
    Includes bibliographical references and index.
    ISBN 0-9634940-6-6 (cloth)

    1. Industrial management. 2. Management. 3. Business. I.
  Brown, David (William David) II. Title

    HD70.U5G64 1995   658
                         QB195-20436

Table of Contents

Acknowledgments

A book of this nature requires considerable assistance by many people before it is completed. We would like to gratefully thank all of the employees at our featured Turbocharged Companies—Southwest Airlines, Chrysler Corporation, Nucor Corporation, The Home Depot, Progressive Corporation, Eastman Chemical Company and SIFCO Forge Group—who so unselfishly gave of their time in helping us understand how their organizations became Turbocharged Companies. Our sincere thanks goes out to John (Jay) Anderson, Sheila Brown, William (Bill) Becker, Jeff Church, Richard (Dick) Damsel, Jeff Gotschall, John Hexter, Moira Lardakis, Bruno Silikowski, Harvey Wiseberg and Garry Zimmerman who carefully reviewed this manuscript and provided many valuable and insightful editorial comments. Thanks as well to Dr. Dorri Jacobs and Laura Bell for their careful review of these words, and their valuable suggestions for the improvement of the final product; and to Adele Fini for her research work, an indispensable part of this book.

Special thanks are due our editor, Mark Kozel, who was so instrumental in the creation of this book. His enthusiasm, creativity and insightful advice provided great inspiration to us on many occasions.

Thanks also to Rachal Rapoport at York Publishing for tirelessly working with us to ensure the best possible product. And to Tina Dracon, our most valuable assistant, for her dedicated and willing support.

Finally, thanks to you, the reader, for thirsting for a way to make your company better than it has ever been.

Larry Goddard
David Brown

This book is dedicated to our children, whose patience, understanding and support during the many hours of work devoted to this project we most certainly appreciate.

Have the Business Success You've Dreamed Of!

Picture the Ideal Company

Imagine, for a moment, that the business you own or work for is so successful that you cannot wait to get there each day. Sure, the challenges that face any business will be there . . . but you and your talented colleagues continue to amaze everyone with your ingenuity and dedication in solving those problems. Sales are better than planned—and have been for some time now. Costs continue to decrease, allowing the company to make money despite a very competitive marketplace, while providing exceptional value to your customers. Everyone is more productive, dedicated and happier than ever before. When customers call and stockholders write—and they do—it is not with complaints, but with compliments. It's almost like a dream.

Let us assure you, a dream it is not. We have just described a business that does not have to be a figment of your imagination— it can be the reality of your organization. And you can transform it! What seems to read more like a script for a fantasy adventure can become reality. You can make your company a place where going to work is a pleasure. Where you and your fellow employees feel good about your work, your company, your product or service. Where your customers consider it a pleasure to do business with you, and your stockholders are pleased with their investment. You can!

It does not matter if you are the CEO, a manager, supervisor, or a line employee of a business that is not performing anywhere near its full potential; you will learn in this book that there are a host of actions you and your colleagues can take to dramatically improve the performance of your company.

Companies just like yours, facing similar problems, with competition just as fierce, have done more than just succeed. Our experience and research, over the last 20 years, has uncovered companies that seem to defy the "status quo." They have risen above a merciless marketplace and delivered sales and profits that others said could not be achieved. They have turned employee boredom, stress and apathy into excitement, creativity and commitment. And they have made their stockholders look forward to the next quarter's report. It is not a fantasy; others, in situations similar to yours, have done it—and so can you.

In 1966, Rollin King and Herb Kelleher had a dream that by offering the lowest possible fares on a shorthaul, no-frills, customer-responsive airline, they could make money. Faced with seemingly overwhelming legal battles from competitors, Southwest Airlines finally got off the ground in June of 1971. From such troubled beginnings, the airline has grown to more than $2 billion in annual ticket sales. During the years 1990-1993, while the rest of the airline industry was losing $12 billion,[1] Southwest earned a tidy $335 million[2]—and had fun doing it! Their employees love to go to work, and passengers cannot seem to write enough complimentary letters.

In 1965, Ken Iverson led the effort to rid Nucor Corporation of all its unprofitable divisions and focus on its one profitable, yet tiny, steel joist manufacturing operation. By 1972 the company had entered the steel making business, competing against such legends as Bethlehem, Republic and U.S. Steel. Using what was then relatively unproven technology, Nucor has since grown to be the fourth largest steel maker in the country. In 1994, Nucor produced seven million tons of steel, generating revenues of nearly $3 billion, and earning profits exceeding $226 million.

In 1990, Chrysler was once again facing bankruptcy. After its bail-out by the U.S. Government in 1980, it had again slid to the brink of financial collapse. The company had fallen to fifth place in the American automobile market, behind Honda and Toyota. Its automobiles were so out of sync with the market, they could only be sold through the use of generous rebates. Even a desperation merger with Fiat fell through. Only four years later, Chrysler set a company record for the number of cars sold and made more money—$3.7 billion—than in any previous year of its history. Chrysler's redesigned minivan, innovative Neon and renovated Ram pickup have all been met with great acclaim. Where its products were once out of step, Chrysler's product offerings are just what the consumers ordered, resulting in an average weighted Return on Shareholders' Equity of 33.6 percent for the three years ended December 31, 1994.

In 1985, Progressive Corporation was a little-known specialty automobile insurer, handling mostly nonstandard policies. Revenues amounted to just over $500 million. Responding to consumer dissatisfaction with the auto insurance industry, Progressive redesigned the company and its products around the needs of the consumer. It developed products and services so that no driver, regardless of record, would have to be turned down for auto insurance, a practice common in the industry. Ten years later, Progressive is the seventh largest US private passenger auto insurer. Progressive's product line covers traditional as well as specialty and nonstandard policies. Revenues in 1994 were just under $2.5 billion, with net profits ringing in at $274 million. The company made an 8.3 percent underwriting profit compared with an estimated industry loss of 9.4 percent.[3] The company's innovative services, including mobile claims "offices" that can be at the scene of an accident in minutes, a toll-free insurance "shopping service," and fast payout on claims, have customers very pleased.

In 1978, Bernard Marcus and Arthur Blank, two recently fired executives of a chain of home center stores, started what would become the world's largest home improvement retailer and one of the 20 largest retailers in the United States. The Home Depot was built on the idea that happy, outgoing, well-trained employees, providing unsurpassed customer service, would make a very successful enterprise for everyone. At the close of fiscal 1994, the company tallied sales of $12.5 billion, with net earnings of $604 million, had 340 stores in 28 states and three Canadian

5

provinces and employed 67,300 employees.[4]   The company is proud to note that an investment of $12,000 in 1982 for 1,000 shares of Home Depot stock would be worth more than $2.5 million[5] today.

Long hidden under the shadow of its former parent, 75-year-old Eastman Chemical Company was finally spun off from Eastman Kodak Company, as an independent enterprise, at the stroke of New Year's 1994. Long an advocate of the unlimited power of the human mind and spirit, Eastman teamed employee involvement with a willingness to work in partnership with its customers. This powerful combination allowed Eastman to close its first year as an independent company with $4.3 billion in sales, achieving net earnings of $336 million. Its performance for that year and the two previous years exceeded that of the average of its peers by over 600 percent.

Southwest, Nucor, Chrysler, Progressive, Home Depot and Eastman—a seemingly diverse group of companies—do have something in common. They defied the odds and succeeded where most of their competitors had disappointing results or failed. They made money in markets, and under conditions, where others said it could not be done. Finally, they have all achieved this by running their businesses, and relating to their fellow employees and customers, in ways that were strikingly similar to one another, yet vastly different from most other companies.

All of the companies we have described so far are large, publicly traded companies about which you undoubtedly have heard. Lest you think that this only works for large companies, we offer the example of the SIFCO Forge Group, a $20 million aerospace manufacturing concern based in Cleveland, Ohio. Much of the original framework that we will reveal in this book was developed as part of our work with SIFCO, starting in the fall of 1993. The Process has since been refined while working with other clients, and through interviews with and studies of other Turbocharged Companies.

At SIFCO, we were searching for a way to "jump-start" the division out of its lethargy. They had been losing money for so long that they were used to it—almost comfortable with it. All the traditional ideas and approaches had been tried, to no avail. Management had written off the employees as roadblocks to productivity and profitability. We realized that our first task was to convince management and the employees that they could turn it around. To achieve this, we felt it was important to provide a *framework* that would allow everyone to understand what they were about to do, while providing a road map with which to gauge their progress.

The board clearly needed to take action. We persuaded them to give our ideas a try. Within months, the losses had stopped. The division returned to profitability, even in a very difficult marketplace, and it has remained profitable ever since. As Barry Fought, SIFCO's Forge Group's CFO puts it, "While we are now at the same sales level we were four years ago, we are doing it with 70 employees in production areas, versus 150 in 1991. We're at 30 employees in the office now instead of 75. Couple those cuts with the productivity gains we have made, and you can see how the red ink disappeared!" The employees are happy, the customers are pleased, and an air of confidence has again returned to this long-suffering company.[i]

Further evidence of SIFCO's "rebirth" was the announcement in June 1995 that industry leader Wyman-Gordon was forming an alliance with SIFCO. This alliance would involve Wyman-Gordon's transferring a significant portion of its forging operation to SIFCO—quite an achievement for a company whose management was ready to throw in the towel only 18 months earlier.

Studying all these companies, as part of the research for this book, allowed us to confirm what we had learned from working with our own clients. These companies match what we have seen in other organizations—organizations that have taken whatever conditions, adversity and problems they were given—and turned them into gold. Companies that have spurned the traditions of the

---

[i] SIFCO Forge Group is a division of SIFCO Industries, Inc., which is traded on the American Stock Exchange.

business world, and in doing so have discovered the secret to their success. Companies that are able to *surge* ahead of their competition, as though they were fitted with a *turbocharger*! We describe them as being a **Turbocharged Company**[i].

The truth is that Turbocharged Companies do not succeed by accident; they do certain things, and create a special environment, that ensures their success. These are very similar to the set of Foundations that we developed in our work with SIFCO Forge Group. We have captured these common elements in what we call the **Turbocharged Company Process**[ii]. This Process is one that any business can follow to become a Turbocharged Company.

To the dismay of the quick-fix crowd, there is no single management technique, or "cure-all," that is behind the success of these companies. Instead, their success is a series of steps that you and your colleagues can easily understand, and competently put into practice. You can, with the material contained in this book, transform your company into a Turbocharged Company!

---

[i] "Turbocharged Company" is a trademark of The Parkland Group, Inc.

[ii] "Turbocharged Company Process" is a trademark of The Parkland Group, Inc.

What's the Common Denominator?

While Turbocharged Companies vary significantly in industry, products or services and size, they do share common characteristics. They all *consistently*

- Outperform their competitors in terms of sales and profits,

and

- Generate superior returns for their stockholders.

And they do it, often without investing inordinate sums of money or adding staff. They do it in good times, and in bad. They do it in high-tech businesses, low-tech businesses, in service sectors, in manufacturing sectors, in commodity businesses and in specialty operations. Most of them are in highly competitive industries. And they are handsomely rewarded for their efforts.

For an example, one need only look at Progressive Corporation, which, in the extremely competitive personal automobile insurance market, generated a three year weighted average Return on Equity (ROE) of 28 percent, almost 74 percent higher than its closest publicly traded competitor. Each year, the company beats its own stretch goal—an ROE 15 percentage points greater than the rate of inflation—by a handsome margin.

Or look at Home Depot, battling the well-known giants in this industry. Home Depot made more money in fiscal 1994 than its public peer group did, in total, from years 1992 through 1994! Its three year weighted average ROE was 50 percent higher than its nearest competitor.

Finally, Nucor Corporation, the steel-making powerhouse, generated a weighted average ROE 50 percent higher than its closest competitor, and was one of only two companies to even be profitable over the last three years. And it did this while investing large sums of money on new technology designed to help the company remain the low-cost leader in the steel business.

Admittedly, these are very high benchmarks to achieve. Nevertheless, they are attainable. We have found a select number of companies that have achieved these high standards—and continue to do so year after year. In the research for this book, **we examined nearly 1,000 of the largest American businesses, and found that slightly more than 3 percent of them qualified as a Turbocharged Company.** A staggeringly small figure—yet we see this not as a condemnation of American industry, but as ample evidence of the opportunities for improvement that exist. Clearly, there are significant opportunities for the other 97 percent to surge ahead of their competitors and join the ranks of the Turbocharged Companies. The members of this exclusive three percent group serve as shining reminders that Turbocharged Company status can be achieved—even in large companies that seem almost too huge to be so nimble in the marketplace. Further, we have seen evidence that if such large, complex businesses can attain this performance level, smaller and more flexible companies can achieve these benchmarks equally well.

Most of the companies that we mention in this work did not start with any special edge—no exclusive patent or other superiority. Instead, each turned what was a level playing field into a competitive advantage. And they did it by applying the **Turbocharged Company Process.** To be sure, they did not call it this, nor did they necessarily follow every step we will outline. Yet each company applied virtually all the principles of the Process, which have given them a decided advantage—or competitive edge. In the face of continuing attacks from their competitors, these companies have the confidence to know that such a competitive edge will not only be maintained, but enhanced.

The telltale measure of a Turbocharged Company, we believe, is Return on Shareholder Equity (ROE). This yardstick of financial performance is calculated by dividing after-tax profits[i] into average shareholder equity (the capital contribution to the business by its shareholders plus accumulated profits that have not been distributed to shareholders). Shareholders of a business expect a return on the equity they invest. It is management's job to maximize the return for their shareholders, who clearly have many investment opportunities and are looking for the greatest return on their funds. Thus, ROE represents a critical benchmark in measuring the financial performance of a business.

Historically, it has been difficult for the entire American business world to keep its ROE above the low teens for long; in fact, it had been stuck at 12 percent[6] for decades. Yet our research has shown that the Turbocharged Companies boast an average weighted ROE of more than 30 percent over the last three years! These are some extremely powerful results.

To qualify as Turbocharged Companies, the businesses went through a careful screening. As a primary criteria for selection, these companies must have outperformed their closest competitor[ii] by more than 40 percent over the last three years. The basis of this analysis was their weighted[iii] average return on stockholders' equity during this same period.[iv] To provide a large enough competitive sample, a minimum of four companies in a particular SIC code were required to be considered for Turbocharged Company status. Finally, any company that experienced a net loss during any of the preceding three years was

---

[i] For purposes of this analysis, we have utilized after-tax profits, before deductions for accounting changes and extraordinary items

[ii] Comparisons made using each company's primary SIC code

[iii] Weightings: most recent year-3; 1 year previous-2; 2 years previous-1

[iv] For purposes of this analysis, the Moody's May 1995 data base was used.

excluded from consideration. For those companies that met this financial benchmark, we then examined each company's operation, to determine if it met the Turbocharged Company criteria. It is only by meeting both criteria that an organization could truly be declared a Turbocharged Company.

We selected several of these companies to feature in this book. Some we have already mentioned, some we have not. We chose companies in varying industries that faced very different challenges, yet that could best illustrate the key principles we were trying to address. Clearly, while we could have mentioned many more companies and used a lot more examples from them, space limitations held us back.

Further, we will also make reference to some companies that may not be on the Turbocharged Company list. This may be because there were not enough competitors in their primary SIC, or another technical reason. Even so, we felt that the work these companies were doing best illustrated certain areas of the Process, and thus we used them.

We have talked considerably about other companies, but how about yours? Wouldn't you like to be able to say that your company outperforms its competitors, and that your company generates superior returns for your shareholders? Of course you would—any businessperson would. We offer you a way to achieve these results that will work—a process that we have tested and proved. It is rational; and it works in companies of all sizes, in all industries, and in all financial situations. If this sounds like what you've been looking for, you have purchased the right book. Read on!

How Do They Do It?

That's the question we get asked most. Ironically, becoming a Turbocharged Company will not be all that difficult for your organization. It does not take manuals as thick as your forearm, nor does it take selling off your present business and starting a new one. It does not take inordinate sums of cash, nor a Ph.D. from Harvard. And, it does not take the "luck of the Irish," or a stream of management consultants.

Based on our own work and research, we have determined that Turbocharged Companies generally share what we call the **Four Foundations.** It does not matter the size of the organization, its location or its competition—or whether it is young or old. What does matter is that Turbocharged Companies all do four important things. They **Unleash People Power, Revere Their Customers, Relentlessly Pursue Productivity, and Dominate Their MicroNiches.**

Right now you may be saying, "Wait. What are these Foundations? What do they mean? How do we implement them?" Rest assured, we will be reviewing all that shortly. Or you may be saying, "That's it? That's too simple!" While the list of Foundations may be relatively short, what each entails is not. None are terribly complicated, but each will challenge you in the way you look at your business, your colleagues and your customers. Finally, once you have had a chance to review the entire Process, it all makes perfect sense. There are no strange sounding steps that demand tremendous leaps of faith to carry out.

The secret is less in the individual steps and more in the entire Process. Becoming a Turbocharged Company is accomplished not by implementing a single foundation successfully, but by ingraining all four into your organization. That's the Turbocharged Company Process.

So, When Should I Start This?

"The time to repair the roof is when the sun is shining"

— John F. Kennedy

Let's face it, the only time you really have control over is today. Yesterday is history, and tomorrow is yet to come. The best of times is today—and today is when you should start the process of transforming your business into a Turbocharged Company. It doesn't matter if your company is in the middle of a financial crisis—there is no better time than today to start turning things around. It doesn't matter if your business is basically sound yet stagnant—today is the time you can begin improving it. It doesn't matter if your company is doing great—today is when you can lay the framework for making it an even better organization. Procrastination alone has probably killed or seriously wounded more companies than competitors and market conditions combined.

Progressive Corporation was not in any financial trouble in 1992 when it decided to change. In fact, the business was going along quite nicely. Yet Chairman Peter B. Lewis and Chief Operating Officer Bruce Marlow knew that the company had to change in order to address policyholders' increasing dissatisfaction with insurance companies. By reducing costs, improving service and giving consumers more control over their insurance purchase, the company felt customers would respond.

And they have. Direct premiums written have increased more than 62 percent in only two years, with profits closely following.

Transforming your business, division, branch, plant or department into a Turbocharged Company will require your commitment to look at your organization in a different light. When you do this, you will realize the potential of a very rich resource that your company always had, but never used to anywhere near its full potential—you and your fellow employees. And, you will clearly see the direct relationship between satisfied customers and bottom line results.

You may be concerned with all the changes that are going to have to be made. It is far easier to stay with that which is familiar. You are probably filled with questions like: What happens if the changes do not work? How do we know we won't make things worse? What happens if we are not up to the task? All these and more are legitimate concerns for people facing the task that lies ahead. Yet we assure you that once you have completed this book, you will discover that the Process is not an overwhelming task, but a series of very logical steps. Many others in your shoes, with no more or less talent than you possess, have inaugurated the Process and have discovered that the upside far outweighs any potential downside.

How Do We Begin . . . ?

The Turbocharged Company Process is a logical series of steps, each building on the one before. As we mentioned, those steps, the Four Foundations of a Turbocharged Company, are:

- **Unleashing People Power**—Creating an environment that stimulates employees to achieve the optimum level of creativity, energy and dedication to the company's goals and success.

- **Revering Your Customers**—Treating customers with the utmost respect, and placing their satisfaction as your company's highest priority.

- **Relentlessly Pursuing Productivity**—Endlessly searching for ways to perform better, faster, more effectively and at a lower cost, and

- **Dominating Your MicroNiches**—Focusing on your strengths and being the best at what you do.

Unleashing People Power is the essential first step. When employees feel good about themselves, their company and the work that they do, they will be in a much better position to **Revere Customers.** Their enthusiasm and positive feelings will be infectious when they talk with present or potential customers. Unleashed employees are a very powerful weapon. They know the company's plans and goals—and how the business is currently performing in relation to those goals. They are fiercely determined to help the company achieve those goals, and the success they bring. Interestingly, the more aggressive the goals, the more determined employees will be.

Unleashed Employees want their company to succeed. They want to know all about their customers. They want to know not only what the customers expect, but what they would appreciate. They want to know how to make the customers' jobs easier and more productive. Their genuine interest and caring attitude will be detected by your customer, who is all the more pleased with his/her decision to purchase your company's product or service. SIFCO's CEO, Jeff Gotschall, echoed this sentiment when he said, "When customers learn you are making changes to better serve their needs, they're flattered. When they get a cheerful, caring voice on the phone, they're impressed. Put those together with quality products, delivered on time, at a reasonable price, and you have a winning combination no customer can ignore."

Once you have Unleashed People Power and truly begun Revering Your Customers, your organization will be poised to begin dramatically improving its productivity. We call this part of the Process **Relentlessly Pursuing Productivity.** You would not want your customers to pay for your own inefficiencies, would you? However, by knowing the needs of your customer, you can reshape your organization into serving them and their market, as efficiently as possible. When your company is Relentlessly Pursuing Productivity, it is constantly searching for ways to do things better—improve productivity, reduce costs and eliminate unnecessary work. The status quo is never acceptable. No matter how efficient your company may get, you will continually be striving to improve. Rethinking each process toward simplification or elimination requires employees who are committed to the goals of your company. And it is those committed employees who keep your customers coming back time after time.

Finally, benefiting from the creativity and enthusiasm of Unleashed Employees who Revere their Customers, and who Relentlessly Pursue Productivity, your company can now move toward **Dominating Your MicroNiche**—being the leader in your field. You will have defined how you will serve the needs of your customer in a particular area—a MicroNiche—and you will become the very best at serving your customers within that arena. While most businesses sell products or services, Turbocharged Companies focus on solving their customers' needs. The reward is becoming the most preferred provider of your product or service, enjoying the increased sales and profits that such status brings.

So you see, the entire process of becoming a Turbocharged Company feeds on itself. The successes in one area enable the next to flourish. Clearly, if Unleashing People Power has not been successfully implemented, it is very unlikely that employees will be in the frame of mind to Revere Your Customers. Similarly, employees will not be inclined to search for every opportunity to Relentlessly Pursue Productivity. Finally, if your company is not Unleashing People Power, Revering Its Customers and Relentlessly Pursuing Productivity, the chances of Dominating a MicroNiche will be significantly reduced.

You might be wondering at this point what the difference is between the Turbocharged Company Process and other management techniques you may have heard about or implemented, *i.e.,* Total Quality Management or "TQM," ISO 9000, Benchmarking, Statistical Process Control or "SPC." While these and other management techniques are valuable, we have found them to have *limited value* when their implementation is not part of a total company process. To be sure, TQM, SPC, ISO 9000 or Benchmarking programs can produce significant results, but they are likely to be disappointing if implemented in an environment that does not Unleash People Power, Revere Customers, Relentlessly Pursue Productivity or Dominate MicroNiche(s). Conversely, when these programs are implemented in a Turbocharged Company environment, their long-term effects are virtually always significantly better.

The Turbocharged Company Process takes a *total approach* to your business. This is the most important point for you to appreciate at this time. The Process focuses on solving the underlying causes that are preventing your company from performing as it could, rather than just treating the symptoms that many other management techniques do. It will not, for example, specifically look at handling your customer service problems more efficiently. Instead, it will redirect your attention to examining the root cause of the customer service problems. Solve that, and the efficiency in handling the remaining problems will increase dramatically.

So, this program is not a fast "cure." It is a thorough process, proven in companies just like yours. We have said it before—you have what it takes to transform your organization into a Turbocharged Company. You have the desire—that's what caused you to buy this book in the first place. You have the tools—they will be outlined in the balance of this book. You have the resources—the people within your own organization.

Much of what you will read here has been written about before. Probably, no single activity in the Turbocharged Company Process is radically different or new. What is very new and singularly unique, however, is the Process itself—how all these techniques tie together to dramatically help your business. The Four Foundations of a Turbocharged Company, applied appropriately and in the correct sequence, are the keys to unlock the huge potential present in your business.

With this understanding of the concepts behind the Turbocharged Company Process, and the details that follow, success is within your reach. Let's begin!

Foundation One—UNLEASHING PEOPLE POWER

THE
<u>TURBOCHARGED COMPANY</u>
PROCESS

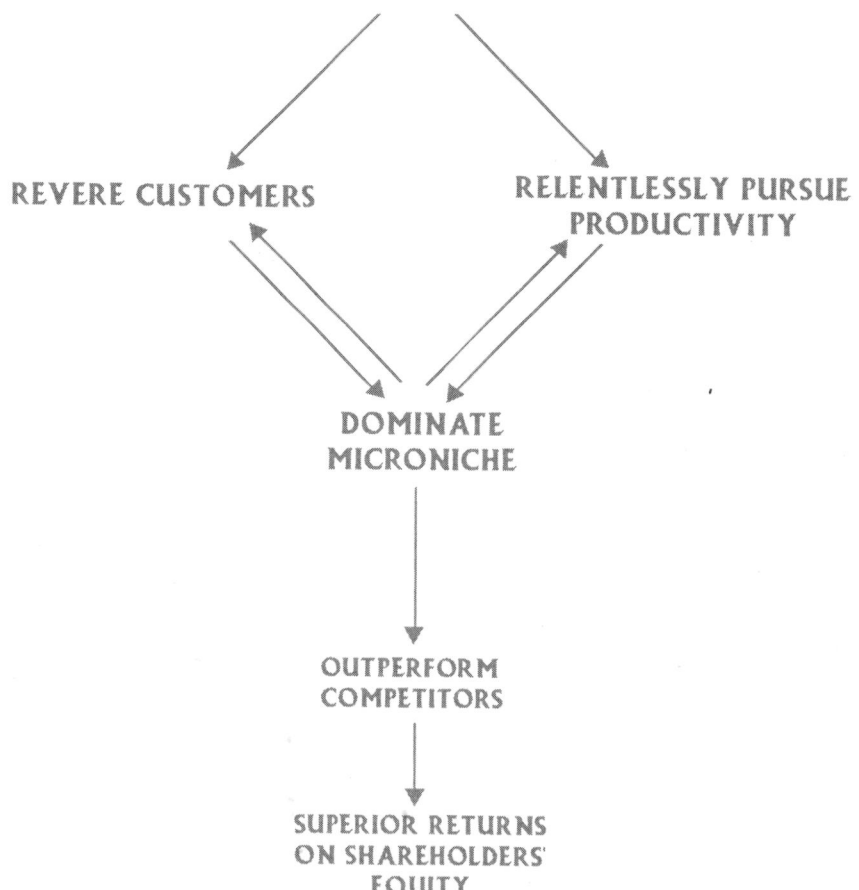

UNLEASH PEOPLE POWER

REVERE CUSTOMERS

RELENTLESSLY PURSUE
PRODUCTIVITY

DOMINATE
MICRONICHE

OUTPERFORM
COMPETITORS

SUPERIOR RETURNS
ON SHAREHOLDERS'
EQUITY

The *graphic on the left illustrates the Turbocharged Company Process, how each of the Four Foundations interact with the other and how they lead to the desired results of outperforming your competitors and generating superior returns on shareholders' equity. It will serve as a guide as we review each of the Four Foundations.*

The first step, as you will discover, is Unleashing People Power—creating an environment that stimulates employees to achieve the optimum level of creativity, energy and dedication to the company's goals and success. It is the key *to Revering the Customer, Relentlessly Pursuing Productivity and Dominating your MicroNiche. You will also see how important it is to Unleash this incredible People Power, and how rewarding it can be to the employees, as well as the company.*

The Secret Weapon

It is rare to read an annual report today where the chairman does not state that "our people are our best asset." While this statement should be true for all businesses, very few are able to achieve the full potential of their people. The culture of most organizations does not facilitate a highly motivated and committed work force, no matter how much management would like to believe otherwise. Employees either do not trust the organization, or do not feel they are being treated fairly, or are still too confused about the company's goals and objectives to be truly unleashed. Simply put, they do not feel any "ownership" in the company or in what the company is trying to do.

Human beings, under the right circumstances, have the potential to achieve levels of productivity and creativity that are often surprising—even to themselves. When *People Power* is unleashed, the results can be staggering. To achieve these kinds of results does not require a work force of superhumans; outstanding results can be achieved with virtually any group of "regular" employees. That is what Unleashing People Power is all about.

It is easy to confuse Unleashing People Power with the management technique called empowerment. Empowerment is commonly described as the process of allowing employees to have a significant degree of say in determining how their work will be performed. While empowerment is essential to Unleashing People Power, there is a whole lot more. To be truly Unleashed, employees must not only be empowered, they must know the company's goals and direction, and its present status in relation to those goals. They will have contributed to the development of the goals. Additionally, Unleashed Employees trust the organization, and have confidence in its future. Unleashed employees work in an atmosphere that fosters talent, teamwork and contribution rather than power, status, and "cover your ass!"

In the competitive environment in which we operate, it is virtually impossible to be a Turbocharged Company if the organization has not succeeded in Unleashing People Power. When People Power is Unleashed, the motivation level of employees is raised significantly—to a level where they *want* to help the company succeed. Herbert D. Kelleher, Chairman, President and CEO of Southwest Airlines, described the feelings of Unleashed Employees this way, "The company's mission becomes the employee's own crusade." Employees develop a positive feeling toward the company which makes them feel it is worthwhile to give that extra bit of effort. Pat Burke, the Engineering Team Leader at SIFCO Forge Group, stated, "People pay a lot more attention to their work. They know every individual's efforts are important."

Unleashed Employees become "Crusaders" for your company, while their counterparts at traditional companies may be "Resisters"—resenting the system that denies them the opportunity to be any more than just another cog in the wheel. Because of this, Resisters lack the energy and vitality to be creative. They do not really want to go out of their way to help the company.

Many ask the reason why. Why do Unleashed Employees become Crusaders, while others become Resisters? The answer resides in the basic motivational instinct—"What's In It For Me ?" It is a question each of us asks ourselves all the time, if not consciously, then subconsciously. Resisters feel the answer is simple, "There's nothing in it for me!" They are frustrated at their inability to effect positive change and see any effort at trying to change things as fruitless. Unleashed Employees, however, answer that question quite differently. They know that their efforts, thoughts and suggestions will make a difference. They can change the organization, making their own future that much brighter. "What's In It For Me?" is answered simply—plenty!

Because of this difference, Crusaders and Resisters are on opposite sides of the spectrum. One is a huge asset, the other a roadblock to your success. Thus, your goal must be to make every one of your fellow employees a Crusader.

When people are totally candid, most will admit that there are times when they just do the bare minimum, and no more, to get the job done. Very few people function anywhere near their peak capacity. Most of us have the ability, under the right circumstances, to be more energized and conscientious. Most employees, perhaps because of the way they have been treated in the past, mistrust their employers. Many expect to be taken advantage of—to be "used." At best, they feel their opinions do not count for anything and probably will not be taken seriously.

This state of mind prohibits employees from going out of their way to help the company. They might do the minimum to get by, and avoid reprimand—but only the very dedicated will go the extra mile. Even more serious, employees who feel this way will often turn a blind eye to any opportunity to help the company. They may even assist in actions to hurt the company, if they believe that their actions, or lack of action, will go undetected. The latter was clearly illustrated in the experiences of a construction products supplier—

> *The company noticed that it was suddenly experiencing a large increase in flat tires on its trucks. When the manager looked into this situation, he discovered that all the flat tires were on trucks that were making deliveries to one particular jobsite. Subsequent examination revealed that the main roadway at this jobsite was strewn with nails that had been carelessly discarded by another trade. When he discussed this with the truck drivers, one of them eventually admitted that while they had seen the nails on the road, they did not make any attempt to remove them.*

When one got down to the real cause of the flat tires, it wasn't accident or coincidence. Simply put, the drivers did not care enough about the company to want to help. They felt no desire or responsibility, to assist the very enterprise that was providing their livelihood. Perhaps, consciously or subconsciously, they wanted to hurt the company for some reason. At $300 or more per tire, they could have saved the company a lot of money. No doubt, if the drivers had owned the trucks themselves, if they were held responsible for the cost of repairs, or if they had wanted to help the company succeed, their attitude would have been completely different.

Turbocharged Companies realize how important it is to create an environment wherein people want to help the company—where they focus their energy and creativity toward the success of the business. Your company may think it can compensate for this by doing a better job *policing* your employees. This is a classic, yet ineffective, approach. Employees have far too many opportunities to do things—or not do things—that can adversely affect the company, yet that will largely remain undetected by any corporate "police" force. Turbocharged Companies realize this. As a result, they focus their energies on Unleashing People Power. Employees who *want* to help the company do not require policing. This approach is certainly far more motivating for employees, and is significantly less costly—and vastly more productive—for businesses.

For example, it is interesting to note that at Nucor, Southwest Airlines and several other Turbocharged Companies, there are no time clocks. As Kathy Pettit, Southwest's Director of Corporate Communications, put it, "Management doesn't watch the clock, so employees don't watch it either."

Additionally, while over 85 percent of Southwest's employees are organized under collective bargaining agreements, the airline enjoys superb relations with all its labor unions. "That's because we all realize we're in this together. We trust management—they're not stealing from us. Herb (Kelleher) gives the employees all the credit for the success Southwest enjoys, and that just builds motivation," states Southwest Airlines pilot Captain Roger Kirchner.

Unleashing People Power is a fundamental prerequisite to becoming a Turbocharged Company. As we said earlier, if a business gets a failing grade in this Foundation, it is unlikely to pass all of the others. Employees who do not want to help the company are unlikely to want to go out of their way to Revere the company's Customers. These customers, sensing the mood of disgruntled employees, will go elsewhere, preferring to deal with companies whose employees display a more positive attitude.

Think of the times you have flown on an airline when the employees just did not seem to care, when they merely seemed to be "going through the motions." Okay, you reasoned, I wanted a discount fare, I guess discount service is part of the package. But then you take a flight with Southwest Airlines. This low-price, high-customer-service, shorthaul airline has completely transformed the traveler's perception of a "discount airline." Southwest's employees are genuinely pleased to have you fly with them—and they show it. In March 1988, Southwest became the first airline ever to win the "Triple Crown"—the best on-time record, best baggage handling and fewest customer complaints in a single month, as reported by the Department of Transportation. Since that time, the airline has not only won the monthly award dozens of times, they have also won the annual award for the last three years! Contrast that with the fact that no other airline has ever been able to win the monthly "Triple Crown" for two or more successive months. Unleashing People Power is fundamental to the "Southwest Spirit"—the airline's legendary customer service and satisfaction.

Most of us, when given the choice, prefer to deal with people who do care. We believe that employees who feel good about themselves and their company will provide better, friendlier and more personable service to customers. Further, the way employees are treated will have a huge impact on their self-esteem and job performance. Co-author Larry Goddard found this out the hard way, very early in his career:

In my first full-time job, as an accountant in a work-study program, I was assigned to report to a partner in the firm. On my first day, I made some kind of mistake in my work (which seemed relatively minor to me). My boss, however, viewed it very differently, and pulled no punches in letting me know. From that point on, from his viewpoint, it seemed I could do nothing right. He repeatedly made it very clear that he believed I was totally incompetent. Within a short period of time, I began to lose most of the abundant confidence I had in myself.

By the time I completed the program three years later, the quality of my work had deteriorated significantly. My motivation and morale could not have been lower. Even worse, I felt any future employment prospects were in serious jeopardy the minute any potential employer found out about my apparent incompetence.

After my graduation, I secured a new job, through a family connection, at another accounting firm. I should point out that it was with great trepidation that I accepted this job. I was sure that it would only be a matter of time until my incompetence was exposed, my family disgraced and my new job lost.

The new firm immediately assigned me to perform the audit of a medium-sized business, supervising a staff of four people. I was quite uneasy, as at the old firm, I had never supervised more than one person. On the first day of the assignment, the partner met me at the client's place of business and introduced me to the owner and his staff. He spent about an hour with me giving some background about the client, and then left. For the next three weeks, I did not see or hear from the partner. I found this a little strange, especially since the partner at the old firm had kept such a close eye on me.

At the end of the audit, the partner returned to review the working papers. He also advised me that, in accordance with the firm's long-standing practice, I would soon receive a written evaluation of my work. You can imagine just how nervous I was waiting the week or so it took for the report to be written and issued. When I finally received it, I was shocked to find out that I had obviously duped him—he had given me an outstanding appraisal. I had exactly the same experiences on my second and third assignments, even though I worked for different partners each time. Both of these partners also gave me outstanding evaluations of my work. Now I really began to wonder—how could I have fooled all of them? Was it just possible that I was not the bungling fool I had been lead to believe I was?

After I became more comfortable with my renewed "competence," I began to analyze why my performance could be so different in the two firms. As I mulled it over, it became clear that the cultures of the two organizations were totally different. The first firm made it clear that they did not trust me, hence their communications to me were negative and demotivating. The second firm, on the other hand, had a much more relaxed and trusting approach. Their positive feedback spurred me to work harder and better.

How many other employees are out there waiting to be released from their "incompetence"? How many people do not believe in themselves because they have been severely criticized too many times—or because they have never been trusted enough to discover their own true potential? Realizing that people can react quite differently when environmental factors change was, without a doubt, the most significant learning experience in our business careers.

If employees are treated as incompetents, they will soon doubt their own abilities. Instead of diving into new work they will hold back, afraid to make a mistake. Before long the employees' main goal will be to avoid doing anything that would irritate anyone.

That was the situation at SIFCO, as Craig Fillinger of the shipping department saw it: "You were scared to death to make a mistake." Fear and oppression replaced creativity and enthusiasm.

Both Bernard Marcus, Chairman, and Arthur Blank, President of The Home Depot once worked for Daylin's Handy Dan Home Improvement Center chain. They were both fired by what Marcus describes as the fire-breathing tyrant of the parent company. "We learned how not to treat people." The two vowed never to treat anyone like they were treated.[7] True to their word, Home Depot employees have the freedom to take their cares, concerns and suggestions right up to the Chairman, if they want.

In organizations where employees are trusted and respected, creativity and enthusiasm flourish. Self-confidence is raised and employees view problems as challenges and opportunities— something that can, should and will be handled. Their attitudes buoyed, employees' excitement and enthusiasm rubs off on customers. Customers sense this "spark" and want to continue to do business with such an organization.

TURBO TIP [i]

Businesses that unlock the secret of Unleashing People Power can achieve a level of energy and creativity that propels the organization to soar ahead of its competitors.

---

[i] "TurboTip" is a trademark of The Parkland Group, Inc.

Where are the Goalposts?

Employees can only be truly Unleashed when they know where the business is heading. Without very clearly defined goals and objectives, employees, even managers, will probably become confused about an organization's priorities. This can lead to a less-than-uniform strategy and a lot of wasted time and resources, resulting in increased frustration for everyone concerned. Unleashed Employees know *where the goalposts are*, and they are committed to getting there.

In a recent survey, the Council of Communication Management found that among 705 employees in 70 companies, 64 percent do not believe what management says, 61 percent do not feel they know enough about company plans, and 54 percent felt decisions were not explained well.[8] Bottom line: Companies cannot assume their messages are clearly being heard and understood.

As we stated earlier, a vital key to unlocking the success of your organization is turning your employees into "Crusaders." This will not be possible, however, until everyone has a clear and unequivocal understanding of the exact company mission.

The mission statement of an organization must define for employees, shareholders, customers, suppliers and other stakeholders where the organization is headed, what it stands for and why it will succeed. While it is tempting to add a lot of words to such a statement, we urge simplicity and clarity as the two essential guideposts. If the most junior person in an organization cannot understand and recite its mission, it is probably not clear enough—and it has not yet been adequately communicated.

Further, employees must have a clear understanding of what it will take to achieve that mission. This understanding must include what their contribution to this mission can and must be.

At Southwest Airlines, the importance of understanding the company's mission is never taken for granted. Executive Vice President, Colleen Barrett, put it this way, "You can't pay lip service to your mission. It is vital that all of your employees know what that mission is. In fact, it's critical to the success of the company. Our mission statement is everywhere in the company. It is taught in every class we hold. Some people have it printed on a card they place in their wallet or at their workstation. Others have it printed on the back of their business cards." James Parker, Southwest's Vice President and General Counsel added, "This is an essential part of Unleashing People Power. If employees don't share the vision, you can't Unleash the Power."

Knowing the mission, or goal, of the organization is of primary importance. But there is much, much more. Chrysler's Mission is "To be the premier North American car and truck company by 1996, and worldwide by 2000." While Chrysler employees know and understand this mission, by itself it is somewhat ambiguous. How will the employees know if they are the premier North American car and truck manufacturer? What does being the premier car and truck company really mean? What impact will this have on stockholders? How are suppliers involved?

To answer these questions, Chrysler has developed what it calls a "vivid description." These are several dozen factors that more clearly illustrate what is meant by being the premier car and truck manufacturer. These "vivid descriptions" include consistently being the lowest cost producer in the industry, having stock price/earnings multiples above the competition and having consumers with a definite bias toward Chrysler. These descriptions qualify the mission statement. They are the markers on the side of the road that let employees, stockholders and the general public know when the company has reached its destination. These markers are just as important to your company, in defining its mission, as they are to Chrysler.

Employees must know the details behind the mission statement. More importantly, they must know how what they do impacts that goal. Knowing the goal is a 20 percent return on shareholders' equity is great—but what does it mean to people? How does their running a machine, their answering customers' calls, or their work in the accounting department impact shareholders' equity? The goal must be stated, but also translated into something to which the audience can relate. If a worker understands that by increasing production from 80 widgets per hour to 100, the company can achieve its goal, the employee is now in a position to do something about it. The goal is now meaningful in the employee's sphere of influence, and he/she can react to that. By stating that increasing collections from 20 percent to 35 percent will achieve this goal, your collections department is then in a much better position to respond. In each case, the employee understands the company's mission, its goals and how his or her individual job affects those goals. With this knowledge, Unleashing People Power provides focused efforts, which leads to desired results.

The employees at Southwest Airlines understand performance measures like "Cost Per Available Seat Mile," "Load Factors" and "On-Time Performance" and realize the direct impact these measures have on the company's mission. They understand the part they play, individually and collectively, in that process. This information is communicated to Southwest's employees on a regular business, for without it, the airline could not achieve the remarkable performance that it does.

It is important, as well, that this information be conveyed in a very open manner. Going up to an employee and stating, "The company needs to make more money, so increase your production by 25 percent" is not going to have the desired results. In fact, it will have just the opposite result. Without the knowledge of why the company needs to make more money, the employee may assume top management wants to make more money for itself.

The employee would undoubtedly see little benefit for himself in that. Or, the employee may assume that someone in "upper management" thinks he or she is loafing—goofing off—and that is the real reason behind the requested increase. The employee, working hard each day, might get quite irritated at this, and may actually slow production down in "retaliation" for this suggestion of laziness.

When the location of the "goalposts" is defined, and total communication is practiced, employees will not only understand what the company is asking—but why. They will then be in a much better position to take the actions within their control, to meet the challenge laid before them. Further, by knowing the whole story, they will be able to suggest alternatives that had not even been previously considered. "We can't get widget production up over 93 pieces, but we did find a way to cut scrap by 65 percent. According to our calculations, that should give us more than the required return." Notice the worker was sure the required return would be there. That is because the employee had information about the company's costs, to which he or she received access during the Unleashing People Power process. In the end, well-informed employees can provide not only what is asked—but more. Unleashed employees are certainly an organization's most important asset.

Employees must also understand the company's tolerance for risk and mistakes, and its attitude toward growth. How much is too much? What happens if you screw up? Knowing this ties in with the last important communication piece: how much a company is willing, or able to invest in new ideas. At most companies, this is a closely guarded secret—cards that management keeps very "close to the vest." Yet employees must know if funds are available to invest in new technology and new processes. Otherwise, they are wasting their time planning for capital improvements to aid production; that the company simply cannot afford. "Spinning your wheels" is the expression most often used to describe this frustrating, and at times humiliating, experience. Informing employees of the company's ability or desire to invest in new methods, processes or equipment is part of the open, trusting relationship that typifies Unleashing People Power.

An organization with a clear mission, well communicated and understood, can devote all its energies to achieving this goal with minimum distraction and deviation. This clarity of purpose provides the platform for developing highly motivated employees, who are focused on satisfying customers and realizing productivity improvements—which are much more difficult to attain in an unfocused organization. Unfocused organizations, by their very nature, spend an inordinate amount of time changing direction, recording false starts and blindly running from one management cure to another. This flurry of seemingly high activity only serves to confuse and demotivate employees, while screening the major underlying corporate problems.

TURBOTIP

"Crusader" employees—who know not only what the "Crusade" is, but also their individual role in achieving it—will ensure that the company achieves its goals.

Remove the Curtain

Unleashing People Power brings with it a need for employees to have basic information about the business. In order for anyone to do a good job, you would expect that person to have access to the information needed to do the job, right? Maybe the following example will help.

How would you like to be on a football team, playing in a stadium that has no yard lines marked on the field, no scoreboard, no line crew and no time clock. To make matters worse, about three quarters of the way downfield, a thick fog settles in. Pretty tough conditions to operate in, wouldn't you say? You have no idea how far it is to the next first down, much less the goal line, and no idea how much time you have left in the game. You think it is fourth down, but you are not sure. You do not know whether to go for a first down, kick a field goal or punt because you have no idea how many yards you've gained. Worse, you do not even know your coaches feelings about running the ball on fourth down and short yardage, rather than punting the ball. You look over to your coach for guidance, but all you get is yelling and cursing.

How effective could you be in such an environment? No matter how good a player you are, you cannot operate in the dark. You must have certain basic information in order to do your job.

Yet isn't that what companies do much of the time with their employees? They are asked to do a job, provided minimal instruction, no feedback, and then get criticized when they do poorly. Don Renkert, a Designer at Chrysler, contrasts the old Chrysler with the new: "In the past, we would spend a lot of time doing sketching and making models, and it would all be for naught. Certain members of upper management would come around and wipe it out—and you didn't know why or what to do next. Now we're involved in every step. Everyone's opinion counts."

When People Power is Unleashed, one of the first things that must be done is to remove that curtain. Employees must have access to company information, so that they can effectively participate. The old-style manager who felt sharing information with employees was a threat to his position or power is an impediment to Unleashing People Power. People have to know enough about the company's operating data and performance in relation to its competitors, in order to help their company thrive in the highly competitive world in which all organizations operate. "Our only restrictions on sharing information are competitive and legal," states Southwest's Associate General Counsel Debby Ackerman. "We share as much operating data as we can with every employee on a daily and weekly basis," she continues.

In the past, information like this was closely guarded, for fear that it might leave the company and provide the competition with vital information. Turbocharged Companies realize that there is inherently less risk in sharing information—and a lot more to gain. Most employees who are trusted with company information, and empowered to use it, will not give it away, for they would be risking their own company—their own jobs. They are much more likely to use it to benefit the company, themselves and their fellow employees.

Providing employees with information about the business, and enabling them to do their jobs more effectively, has another significant benefit. Showing employees that they are trusted with important information makes them feel flattered and pumped up. "Gee, the company respects me enough to trust me with this information," will be the response. This type of environment is very motivating to employees and is a valuable key to Unleashing People Power.

With this information must come education. Few employees will understand Efficiency, Profit Margins, Inventory Turns, Return on Equity, Net Income or any of the other measures of a company's performance. Once they do, however, they are in an unparalleled position to take the steps necessary to improve the company. "Enlightened Self Interest" we call it. It works!

When employees have the information—and the knowledge about understanding and using this information—they will have the tools they need to do their jobs more effectively. They can see first hand the impact their actions have on the company's performance. They can see where the bottlenecks are and can use their creativity and energy to solving those problems. By sharing information with other employees, you have unlocked one of the fundamentals to Unleashing People Power.

TURBOTIP

Corporate Crusaders, traveling in the dark without a roadmap, will get disoriented, disillusioned and lost. Give employees the information they need to do their jobs more effectively.

Abandon Command and Control Management

The changes in management style required to transform your organization into a Turbocharged Company can be very significant. In many cases, these changes conflict with the beliefs that managers were previously encouraged to hold, in order to be successful. The classic management technique of the past has been along the military style concept of "Command and Control." Under this management style, it is solely management's responsibility to develop the company's strategies and direction. Workers are only told *what* to do—and seldom told *why*. They have little, if any, input concerning the direction the business is headed, or the way things are to be done. Reflecting on the old Chrysler Corporation, Clyde Quillen, a team leader on the manufacturing line, states, "You could give a monkey six bananas a day to do the job we were doing. You didn't have to think."

The old approach may have worked well when markets evolved more slowly and products could take years or decades to develop. In today's fast-paced, competitive environment, however, no such luxuries exist. Companies with a brilliant product idea that cannot quickly and cost effectively bring it to market are just as doomed as the company that never gets the brilliant idea in the first place. Jack Welch, the CEO of the General Electric Corporation, flatly told his managers that the company cannot afford management styles and practices that suppress and intimidate, and that managers would have to change their styles in order for the company to advance.[9]

If your company still subscribes to the traditional Command and Control management style, such practices will have to be discarded for People Power to be truly Unleashed. We realize that this concept may be quite concerning to some. Does management simply abdicate all its responsibilities and abandon the company to the employees? Not at all—yet the fundamental role of managers in the organization must change. Instead of issuing directives, managers must sketch out the mission and related tasks, and then allow employees sufficient freedom to carry these out. Instead of controlling every facet of a project, managers must ensure employees have the resources, information and support they need to be successful. They monitor the entire project, not every detail. As Chrysler's Chairman and CEO Robert J. Eaton puts it, "Management is responsible for the *what*, and the employees are responsible for the *how*."

Further, management's role becomes more that of a coach than a "boss." The manager works with each employee to recognize and reward individual achievements that will help the group as a whole improve its performance. At times, this recognition may be in the form of an "atta-boy" for a specific achievement. Or it may take the form of group recognition, or even some form of tangible recognition of the individual's progress. The manager now functions as a resource to help employees become all they are capable of. Kathy Pettit, of Southwest Airlines, contrasts recognition at Southwest with that of her former employer, Braniff Airlines: "At my former employer, you only got recognition if you screwed up. If you did something great or heroic, you never heard a word. At Southwest, when you get a compliment from a customer, the customer gets a thank you letter and the employee gets a note from Herb Kelleher."

To be sure, this new management style will facilitate substantial "flattening" (reduction of layers of management) of your organization, as managers can generally coach more employees than they can "Command and Control." When employees are Unleashed, they simply require considerably less supervision—

they are motivated to supervise themselves. We are rapidly approaching the days of those that plan and those who do—with no need for those who were in the middle. This "delayering" of an organization stimulates improved communication between senior management and line workers, which can further reduce operating costs.

Nucor, the nation's fourth largest steel producer has only four levels of management from the chairman to the entry-level worker. As CEO Kenneth Iverson puts it, "If the janitor gets four promotions, I'm out of a job!" In Nucor's case, this scant management is underscored with a home office staff that is a minuscule 23 people—not bad for a $3 billion company!

In order to effectuate dramatic change in their organization, Chrysler's management made a major shift in the company's organizational structure. The change was based on the recognition that while traditional organizations are structured vertically, actual work processes generally flow horizontally. Chrysler found that its vertical structure resulted in independent departmental fiefdoms (which they termed "chimneys").

As shown in figure 1, each of these chimneys operated in complete isolation from the cares and concerns of any other department. The designers would come up with an idea, having no first-hand information on whether the design could be built on a cost-effective basis. They just "did their thing" and "tossed it over the wall" to the next department. Anywhere along the way, the entire process could become derailed when problems occurred, forcing the project to drop back a department or two. The end result was a very costly and time-consuming way to produce an automobile.

Chrysler's Platform Team concept changed all that. Introduced in the late 1980's, Chrysler reorganized away from its vertical structure to 4 teams, each responsible for a different type of vehicle (Small cars, Jeep/Truck, Minivan, and Large car). As figure 2 shows, instead of having separate fiefdoms, all the designers, engineers, purchasing staff and manufacturing experts for each Platform Team were gathered in one area.

CHRYSLER'S SHIFT IN AUTOMOTIVE DEVELOPMENT WORK METHODS

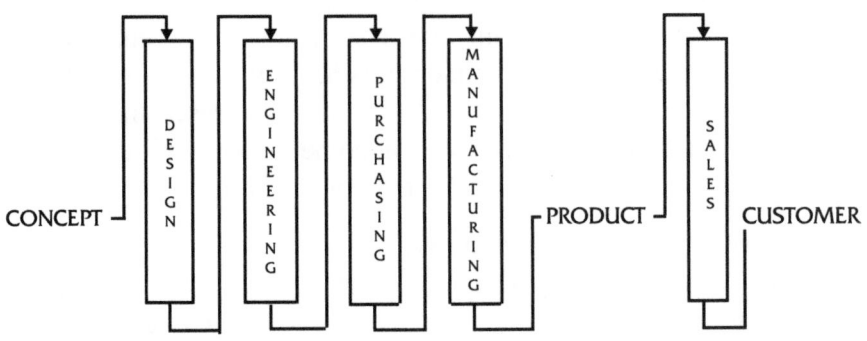

VERTICAL WORK STRUCTURE (CHIMNEYS)
(Figure 1)

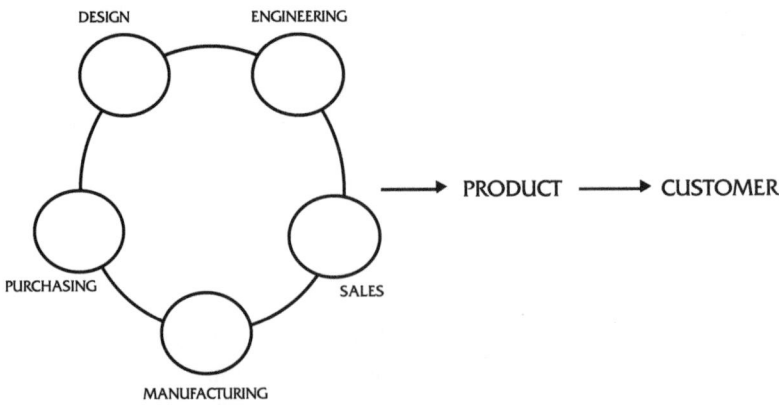

HORIZONTAL WORK STRUCTURE (PLATFORM TEAMS)
(Figure 2)

Everyone on the Platform Team was working toward the same goal—the finished automobile. If an engineer had a problem, he could talk with the designer at the next desk. The engineer could consult with purchasing and manufacturing on the best way to build a particular part or feature. In short, people worked as a team instead of in a function.

The results have been dramatic. Chrysler has essentially cut in half the amount of time it takes to move an automobile from idea to finished, saleable product. In large measure, this can be attributed to the work of Platform Teams, the horizontal work structure, and a different management style.

Certainly, changing from the old, tried and true management style to the new does bring with it some difficulties and a degree of discomfort. Change is difficult for most people. Elimination of positions is never a pleasant task—but certainly an essential one. Further, those middle managers remaining in the organization will need to be retrained as team leaders or coaches. Current studies indicate 15 percent will take to it like ducks to water, 15 percent will never see the light and 70 percent will need a lot of coaching and counseling in order to make this change.[10] Everyone should understand that the skills needed—patience in sharing information, trust in letting others make decisions, and the ability to let go of power—cannot be put on as easily as yesterday's clothes. These skills take time to develop. Yet it must, of necessity, be "learning on the go." The business cannot afford to wait to make the changes necessary to unleash its greatest resource—its employees.

There will need to be sensitivity to the fact that some managers will be uncomfortable with these changes. After all, they are the ones giving up something previously granted to them—power. In this new environment, managers will instead have to earn respect. Workers, operating in this new environment, will be gaining respect, involvement and self-esteem. It is very exciting for workers, yet can be very threatening for managers.

The CEO's role in counseling managers on their new roles, while providing the training they need, will be quite important.

Managers will be looking for a lot of reassurance. As we've mentioned, hardly anyone likes change. Some managers, clearly in new, and for them, uncharted waters, may fervently want to return to the "old ways." The CEO's strength in staying the course is essential. Coaching and counseling these managers will help them adapt to this new environment. It is often advisable, even necessary, to secure the services of an outside facilitator, experienced in these issues, to assist in this process.

At Southwest Airlines, Executive Vice President and Chief Operations Officer Gary Barron sums up management's role this way, "The purpose of management is to support line employees. Our sole purpose is to make it easier for those folks. We don't fly the airplanes, we can't work the ticket counter—only the people in the field can make us a success."

That kind of perspective certainly makes the old Command and Control structure look pretty bleak, doesn't it? Nucor, Southwest, Progressive Corporation, Chrysler, The Home Depot, Eastman Chemical Company, SIFCO Forge Group and many other corporations have realized that by working with employees—giving them the resources and support to translate a mission into reality—develops the most powerful competitive force they have. Instead of forcing employees into the robotic state of the Command and Control structure, they have Unleashed People Power to let their corporations soar.

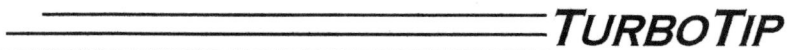

TURBOTIP

"Commanded and Controlled" employees will "do as they are told," yet they will do a lot more if they are encouraged and guided by inspirational leaders.

Involve Employees

The easiest way to raise the self esteem and motivation of employees is to involve them in the business. Employees who are invited to participate in planning, developing strategies and searching for new ideas and better methods usually respond with vibrant enthusiasm, once they get over their disbelief that the company really wants their input. Allowing, indeed expecting, employees to make and implement decisions on their own is one of the most profitable things a company can do.

When employees are treated as just sets of *hands* hired to do a task, they will respond and behave accordingly. When, however, employees are encouraged to apply their *minds* toward improving quality and productivity or reducing waste, the results can be astounding.

Companies that learn this important lesson develop a huge advantage over their competition. Southwest Airlines regularly has competitors in to study the airline's "Best Practices." These competitors are astonished that they would be permitted to do such a thing. Herb Kelleher knows that his competitors can copy some of the physical attributes and techniques, but Unleashing the hearts and souls of employees is not something that can be duplicated without a total commitment to Unleashing People Power and all that it entails. "Other airlines just don't have faith in their own employees; that's why they can't emulate Southwest," states Cleveland Station Manager Jeff Murrin. Unleashing People Power is such a powerful tool—yet only

Turbocharged Companies can see it. To everyone else, it is an invisible myth—they have heard about it but have never experienced it first hand. They are not sure it really even exists. Rest assured, myth it is not. It is real, it is powerful, and you can capture it to make your business soar!

At Chrysler Corporation, encouraging employee involvement has become a way of life. Like any company with industrial sites, Chrysler had factories with soil that, over years of use, had become contaminated. A group of employees from Chrysler's Environmental and Energy Affairs Department found a user-friendly solution to this problem. Working with an outside vendor, the group discovered that the soil could be converted into bricks, and that in the brickmaking process, all the contaminants are destroyed. Forty million bricks later, everyone was happy.[11]

In the very early days of Southwest Airlines, the company had four airplanes and was growing quite fast. At the same time, it was also strapped for cash, and so had reluctantly found a buyer for one of the planes. Everyone got together to discuss the situation, and the general consensus was that Southwest would have to cut back the schedule of flights. But the rank and file employees said "No!" They figured if they could turn the airplanes around at the terminal faster, the company could keep the same flight schedule with 25 percent less aircraft. Thus was born Southwest's 10 minute turnaround, and the Southwest Spirit. The airline allowed its employees to use their minds in dealing with a very serious dilemma facing the company, and the employees threw their hearts and souls into developing a solution that would not only help with the immediate problem, but also provided a major competitive advantage, fueling the company's subsequent explosive growth.

Finally, Turbocharged Companies actively involve employees in planning for the future. In the past, this has been the private domain of management. Workers were given instructions but were rarely informed of the background behind the decisions, or how they fit into an overall plan. By involving employees in all phases of planning, your company can enjoy a synergy never before realized. First, better decisions will be made because the people responsible for day-to-day implementation can help mold the plan around the practical realities that are often unknown to management. Second, and most important, with "ownership" in the plan, employees are much more likely to give the energy and attention it takes to make the plan a reality. It is a classic win-win situation.

Involving employees in the business provides the creativity and vitality needed to energize the organization. It facilitates the discovery of creative solutions to problems facing the company. It makes employees feel better about themselves—and more committed to helping their company succeed.

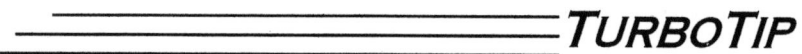*TURBOTIP*

When employees are allowed to use their minds along with their hands, there is a very good chance they will throw their hearts and souls in with the package—at no additional cost to the company.

Establish Work Teams

With the decline in effectiveness of Command and Control management, Turbocharged Companies are increasingly, and effectively, using teams to achieve breakthroughs in performance. As competitive forces continue to erode profit margins, it simply becomes less effective to rely on the skill and ingenuity of managers and supervisors alone to generate ideas and strategies to stay ahead of the competition. To achieve the kind of unique breakthroughs for which companies like yours are searching, a new kind of energy is needed.

Turbocharged Companies make extensive use of work teams throughout their organizations. Work teams are simply a group of individuals put together to solve a particular problem, work on a particular process or product, or run a certain operation within an organization. The synergy, energy and creativity they bring to a situation can be incredible.

Southwest Airlines was experiencing an abnormally high employee turnover rate in one location. (Southwest's turnover rate is normally much lower than industry averages.) This turnover situation created another huge problem, as it left very few employees at the location with any significant amount of experience with the airline. High turnover lead to workers putting in double shifts for weeks at a time, which lead to employee burn-out. Predictably, all this resulted in a significant increase in customer complaints.

Southwest needed to find a way to instill its culture into this station, but lacked people with enough experience to talk about culture, much less instill it. The solution was to form a team of experienced employees from throughout the Southwest system. This team physically relocated to the troubled station for six months, and was charged with instilling the Southwest Spirit at that station. While team members did not know one another, they knew their airline and their culture, and exactly what needed to be done. Their presence would not only facilitate instilling the Southwest Spirit, but would provide local management with a breather from the day-to-day "putting out fires" routine. Within two months, the team's work began to bear fruit. The complaints turned to compliments, as 99 percent of the letters received were positive!

A team, as its name describes, is a group of employees who work together either on a regular or project basis, and where all team members function as equals. Members of the team can vary from production workers, clerks or accountants to managers, sales people or customer service representatives. Most teams do have a team leader, but the team leader is not the "boss" of the group. The team leader usually functions as a coordinator, scheduling meetings, getting needed information and helping guide the team when it is stumbling or veering off course. Your team leaders should function like "player coaches." For the vast majority of the working day, the team leader functions as a "player," performing regular value-added functions. When the team needs guidance, coordination or focus, the team leader takes on the additional role of facilitator. This type of team is known as a "self-managed" or "self-directed" work team.

Not all teams that exist in Turbocharged Companies are self-managed. Some, like Chrysler's Platform Teams, are headed by a Vice President. Yet even in those teams, the "leader" does not manage. His job is to sketch out the "charge" of the group—what they are to do—then step back and let them do it. Robert Eaton, Chrysler's Chairman, states, "[Once they get their assignment,] they go away and do it, and they don't get back to us unless they have a major problem. And so far, they aren't getting into major problems."[12]

While team leaders are often members of the management team, this is not always the case—nor should it be. At Turbocharged Companies, it is the person with the best coaching and facilitating skills that is usually chosen to be the team's leader. The leader may be a manager, or a non-manager, and may even be an hourly worker. The old "rank" does not matter—helping the team achieve its objective does. That's the difference.

The lesson here for traditional managers is learning that People Power does not mean capitulation or abandonment. It is just the *what* and *how* of their jobs that changes, as the focus shifts to communication, coaching and consensus-building. It requires developing a tolerance for mistakes, because they will happen. For it is only by those mistakes that people learn and grow.

To be sure, all Turbocharged Companies retain a top management structure. Yet here as well, changes are made. While top management retains the ultimate responsibility and authority for decision making, these companies rely heavily on team involvement. Teams provide the creativity, new ideas and productivity breakthroughs vital to a Turbocharged Company. Our observations confirm that, in most Turbocharged Companies, over 90 percent of the recommendations made by such teams are accepted and implemented. Senior management, while retaining the ultimate veto power, is seldom required to exercise this right. And this creates an excellent balance within an organization. Employees feel motivated because they have a material say in how the organization is run. At the same time, management feels more relaxed because they have not given up their right to make a decision.

When employees get over the initial unfamiliarity with self-managed teams, it is our experience that they generally become substantially more motivated and creative. Most people thrive when given the opportunity to become involved in helping the company improve. They have more freedom, but along with it, they also get additional responsibility. They take ownership of the problems they eschewed in the past, and take the seemingly overwhelming steps necessary to solve them.

At Kodak, teams have had a profound effect on the organization. One team was facing a problem with bad batches of film emulsion that seemed to have everyone stymied. Three team members worked on their coffee breaks and lunch periods to try to solve the problem. The problem was traced back to some melting kettles, which were in an area that could not be monitored via Kodak's traditional means. Undeterred, the team salvaged some computer gear and wires destined for the scrap pile. They fashioned a real-time monitoring system that could help solve the melting problems as they occurred. This monitoring was so successful, Kodak eventually replaced it with a state-of-the-art system.[13] The lesson here is clear—when employees feel the welfare of the company, hence their destiny, is in their own hands, no problem is unsolvable.

In the early stages of a team's life, things move slowly. It takes some time before the team members are comfortable with each other, their task and their newfound autonomy. The first few meetings usually involve a lot of exploratory talking with very little result. The group may begin to grow anxious, feeling they should be doing something. It is during this time that the team leader plays a crucial role, assuring the team members that this phase of team development is normal. As the group gets more comfortable and relaxed with itself, ideas usually start to flow.

Effective self-managed teams develop an ability to brainstorm freely. Members, through their early exploratory meetings, now feel confident to express their ideas without fear of ridicule or embarrassment. This is extremely important because most breakthrough ideas start off sounding a little strange, incomplete and often just plain off-the-wall!

Our experience with teams has been very exciting. We have witnessed groups of people transformed from apathetic to highly creative and motivated. Under the old Command and Control management system, only very talented managers had the ability to motivate people in this way. We have also witnessed the positive interaction between people at all levels of a company, including salaried, hourly and unionized employees.

Teams, like any other management strategy, are not without their pitfalls. Team members do not always get along, some people abuse the privilege of being on a team, and some who are not selected to serve on a team resent those who are. As previously mentioned, supervisors often have the hardest time learning to become a team player, wherein they earn respect because of their contribution rather than their position. All of these hurdles, and more, can and will be overcome. We will attempt to provide you with help for these situations within this text and also in Appendix "A," located in the back of this book. It has been our experience, however, that patience, perseverance to the task at hand and complete honesty with the group will be the tools used most often in resolving such difficulties.

Hopefully, we have convinced you that work teams are important. You have seen the impact they have had on other organizations. Now, you wonder, how do you go about setting these teams up? In Foundation Three, you will find more descriptions of the workings of teams—both on a process and a project basis. There you will see the immediate impact teams can bring and how they function.

But we do think it is important, here, to state some basics about Unleashing teams in your organization. First, work teams must be empowered by the CEO to perform a specific function or review a specific area. This empowerment must not only include the CEO's support, but the support of all senior management.

Second, teams must be empowered to make a change. At GE, "Work-Out" teams (GE's terminology for a self-managed work team) meet, dissect, examine and recommend change to management. Management, however, must respond immediately to the suggestions made by the Work-Out Team.[14] The worst thing that can happen to a team is that their recommendation falls on deaf ears, or gets studied to death. Teams do not exist to publish tomes, they exist as the agents of change.

Whenever possible, the team should be empowered to implement their plans without coming back to management for approval. If management has clearly defined the mandate and the scope of the team, it is unlikely that the team is going to implement an action that would be detrimental to the company. So, why bog down teams with waiting for management's blessing? What value will be added to their work? Our experience has shown that the motivation of Unleashed Employees usually produces results that far exceed any conceivable risk.

There will, however, be circumstances where the decisions to be made by the team are of sufficient importance, affecting other teams or the direction of the company. In this situation, it may be more prudent to require the team to secure management's approval prior to taking any action.

When the team is created, it is essential that the team members, and senior management, have a clear understanding of the team's power to implement. If prior approval is necessary, senior management must ensure a speedy review and approval process, and be sensitive to the feelings of the members of the team.

Third, teams cannot exist in a vacuum. They need input from all affected areas in the organization. They need to bring workers and managers "into the loop" so that the feasibility of the solution, and its implementation, are assured.

It is helpful, even desirable, for teams to have a "management sponsor"—a member of senior management that can act as a liaison between the team and management. This sponsor can help the team communicate its ideas, as well as assist in securing the resources necessary to implement the team's plans successfully. In order to be an effective supporter of the team, however, the sponsor must be kept well-informed of the team's activities.

Fourth, teams need a seemingly impossible task (yet one they can get their arms around) with a tight deadline. This fosters the creative thinking necessary to make really major breakthroughs. If there were plenty of time, the problem could be studied to death. If the problem is too easy, an "off-the-shelf" solution would work. But if the task seems impossible, and the timetable short, the "off-the-shelf" ideas get dumped and the real work begins. The results can be incredible.

Chrysler's President and Chief Operating Officer, Robert A. Lutz, illustrates this point with a story about some junior-level Chrysler people who were trying to reduce, by 10 percent, the company's expense on "hygienic paper"—more commonly referred to as toilet paper and hand towels. But how do you reduce this type of expense—ask employees to go to the bathroom 10 percent less often? Hardly—instead, a cross-functional team looked at hygienic paper buying not just at their facility, but throughout the corporation. By consolidating purchases from dozens of suppliers to just one, the team saved 50 percent of Chrysler's previous annual expenditure on such items. And employees can still go to the bathroom as often as they want![15]

Finally, understand that mistakes will happen. As humans, we are bound to make them. Teams need to know this, and to know that even in mistakes, some lessons are learned. For if we cannot learn from our mistakes, then we are doomed to make the same ones over and over again.

Turbocharged Companies have learned that the use of teams can greatly enhance their ability to generate creative and responsive solutions to the challenges and obstacles they face. Replacing the hierarchical structures of the past, the interactivity of teams not only allows the company to grow, they are highly stimulating to employees and a natural part of Unleashing People Power.

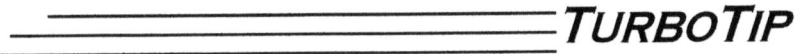

TURBOTIP

The collective energy and creativity of a group of individuals, functioning in an environment of equality and mutual respect, will exceed that of any single individual virtually every time.

Nurture Self Esteem

Much has been written and recorded on the subject of motivating employees. Can management do it, or must it come from within each employee? Is it money, recognition, incentive or acclaim? The debate goes on and on. We believe that treating employees with dignity and respect is the first step in nurturing self-esteem. Employees must feel good about themselves before they can feel good about management and the business. At SIFCO, we witnessed a very poignant example of how important this is.

At the start of our engagement, we talked with every employee in small groups of 10 or less. When we were interviewing a group of unionized hourly workers, one of them, a long-time veteran, described in distressing detail how the company made him feel.

He said that when he walked into the company's gates in the morning, he felt like he was entering a prison camp, where he was serving a sentence "for a crime committed by management." With tears in his eyes, this 60-year-old man described the indignity he felt from the unfair treatment and lack of respect handed out by management. He recounted the insecurity he felt—because he was aware of the company's adverse financial performance. He deeply resented and was confused by management's accusations that workers like himself were to blame. As he spoke, the other nine

61

workers in the group sat there, nodding their heads in somber agreement, obviously sharing his pain.

When we subsequently met with the division management (who are no longer with the company) to get their assessment of the reasons for the company's demise, they attributed it to events totally beyond their control. The major reason, in their opinion, was a depressed market for their products. Inadequate and outdated equipment also received some blame. When we asked if employee motivation was a factor, they responded that they had tried to motivate the employees. Their efforts proved futile because, in their opinion, the workers were basically lazy.

With this and other information, we made our presentation to the company's board of directors. We advised them of our belief that the division management's Command and Control style was having a serious and detrimental effect on the business. In addition to several other changes, we recommended changing to a more open, team-oriented management approach—where all employees are treated with respect and equality. The board approved the changes, which were immediately implemented. Within one month, productivity increased 30 percent, and worker grievances virtually disappeared. Twelve months later, the company's progress continues. After years of substantial losses, SIFCO is again enjoying profitability, and the morale of all the employees remains high. The keystone of this turnaround was Unleashing People Power—letting the employees do what they knew had to be done, and allowing them to feel good about themselves and their contribution to the company. SIFCO demonstrated that the leverage of People Power has in making a company more efficient, productive and responsive.

The SIFCO success story started by recognizing the importance and contribution of every employee. Great efforts were invested in reaching out to all employees and including them in the process. The company then "leveled" with the employees. "This division has been losing money for a long time, and if we can't turn it around, the board of directors will probably vote to sell it," proclaimed Hudson Smith, Division General Manager, in a meeting with all employees. The employees were then invited to participate in the process of finding ways to make the division a Turbocharged Company.

Despite years of conflict with management, these employees, salaried and hourly, responded with an energy and dedication to purpose never before seen. They served on teams, came forward with ideas, uncovered ways to do things better and did whatever it took to achieve the division's new goals. They were able to focus on achieving these new goals because, for the first time in the company's history, the operating performance information was shared with each and every employee. By ten o'clock every day, each employee knew the orders, shipments, productivity and several other key statistics from the previous day.

Armed with this information, and the desire to help the company succeed, these employees made things happen. When productivity dropped off, orders were thin, scrap rates were out-of-line or just about anything else was not going according to plan, the employees got together. They discussed the problem and inevitably came up with a solution. Often these problems seemed virtually insurmountable, but the employees would not be deterred. After a few successes, they began to thrive on achieving the impossible. They did it through teamwork and persistence; they just would not give up!

When they embarked on this venture, none of the SIFCO employees believed they could achieve what they eventually did accomplish. This is the beauty of Unleashing People Power: the employees exceeded even their own ambitious expectations—and by a long shot.

Once this level of People Power was achieved, the employees turned their attention to Revering Their Customers and Relentlessly Pursuing Productivity. Customers immediately noticed the change in the company, and rewarded it with a large increase in orders. Productivity levels increased over 30 percent within the first ninety days. Nine months after the start of the Process, Unleashing People Power had transformed SIFCO Forge Group from a corporate financial drain to a unit poised to regain its profitable industry leader status once again.

Had we stuck our heads in the sand and agreed with management that the employees could not be motivated, the SIFCO Forge Group would not be around today. But, because we believed in the Power of People and what that power can bring to an organization, the story is quite different. And that success is reflected in the broad smiles of the SIFCO employees—smiles generated from pride, satisfaction and regular receipt of some fairly sizable bonus checks!

Employees who feel good about themselves, and the contribution they can make in an organization, are capable of doing far more than employees whose self-worth has been destroyed by past management practices. A company must help employees gain their self-esteem so that the employees can help the company achieve its goals.

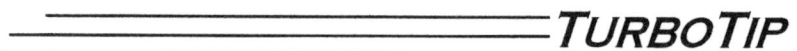

TURBOTIP

Building and preserving the self-esteem of every employee is one of the most inexpensive activities a business can undertake, yet it has the potential to yield the most lucrative rewards.

Get Rid of the Roadblocks

To truly Unleash People Power, the pecking order and associated perks that often accompany Command and Control structures have to be eliminated. In a Turbocharged Company, everyone is treated equally. Sure, some people have more responsibility than others, and they are compensated accordingly. Yet Turbocharged Companies work hard to create an environment where everyone's contribution is valued and appreciated, for every role is vital to the success of the enterprise.

While treating everyone equally is easily stated, changing the "I deserve this" attitude that pervades the management thinking of most traditional companies is a formidable obstacle to Unleashing People Power. Consider this:

As we previously mentioned, we were called in to help the SIFCO Forge Group. When we studied the company, we discovered that it could not only survive, but excel. To do this, however, would require some substantial changes. The first change was Unleashing People Power.

The newly created management team had pledged to work side-by-side with employees in manufacturing, sales, customer support, and all other areas of the business. It was to be "all for one and one for all." Or so we thought....

On the way into the building a day before the speeches were to be delivered and all the changes made, we observed an immediate impediment to the plan. As each employee rushed from the back end of the parking lot to make the 6 a.m. starting whistle, they ran past a row of empty parking spaces, right in front of the building. The executive parking lot would not be filled this early in the day—not for another several hours. So, while the employees parked in the general lot where the best spots went to those who arrived earliest, the executives had reserved spots. The Chairman could come in at 9 o'clock and still be assured of his parking space right next to the door. Somehow, this did not equate to "one for all and all for one." The we *and* they *distinction was still alive and well.*

We approached the Chairman, Chuck Smith, and the CEO, Jeff Gotschall, with a simple request. Management needed to give up their reserved parking spots for someone more important—the customers. After all, they had to walk past those same empty reserved spaces too. It was pretty obvious to Chuck and Jeff that if they *weren't prepared to back up their "new order" at the company with their actions, they were not going to achieve any credibility with their employees. After all, the employees had heard the rally speeches before. What was going to make this one different— believable? They agreed. Before the big meeting convened the next day, a huge outdoor banner was strung across the executive parking lot, proclaiming it the Customer parking lot. From that day on, the executives parked in the same general parking lot as every other employee. It sent a powerful message through the organization, as well as to customers. We are convinced that this was an important spark that fired the dramatic turnaround that subsequently evolved.*

When you take actions seemingly as mundane as this one, you follow the first rule in believability, which, according to Colleen Barrett, Executive Vice President of Customers at Southwest

Airlines, is "walking the talk." It was no longer a "do as I say, not as I do" message. In that singular action, management supported their words with action.

Other organizations, when starting the Unleashing process, make even more radical changes. Consider the elimination of "Mahogany Row." Intel Corporation did just that—CEO Andy Grove has a cubicle, not a private office.[16] Instead of his managers occupying traditional offices, they have a cubicle just like everyone else. It sends a message to all employees—we are all equal. Similarly, executive dining rooms, country club memberships, stadium loges, first-class travel and all the other trappings of upper management must go.

At Nucor, base salaries of top executives are lower than at most other companies. Further, they have no employment contracts, no profit sharing pension, no discretionary bonus and no retirement plan. In fact, management's benefits are no better than those of any other employee, and management is even excluded from certain benefits paid to other employees. Top execs are paid a bonus based upon return on shareholders' equity, just like most employees are paid productivity bonuses. If the company does well, the executive bonus can be very lucrative, yet if the company does poorly, the bonus can be zero. When John Correnti, Nucor's President, walks through a plant working only three days a week due to low volume, the employees know his pay has been cut as well. "Can't you see how important that is to our employees? Every single one of them knows that if their pay is cut, the managers' and officers' pay is cut back even more. It's called share the gain, share the pain."

While we always advocate elimination of the perks that separate management from every other employee of the company, we also stress that care must be taken in this process. Elimination of perks can be viewed as taking something away from a manager, who may consider them part of his/her overall remuneration. In this event, exploration of increased bonus opportunities or other incentive packages may provide a possible solution.

Finally, seemingly mundane things like dress can be an effective roadblock to success. We have noticed that in most Turbocharged Companies, dress codes are relaxed. Somehow the elimination of the suit and tie just seems to make communication easier. When Chairman Bernie Marcus and President Arthur Blank of The Home Depot visit one of their stores, which they do very frequently, they remove their suitcoat and tie and instead don one of the same orange work aprons every other employee wears. And, they expect their division presidents to do the same. It helps them get closer to the customer and the employees, the source of 75 to 80 percent of the ideas implemented each year.[17] Southwest Airlines, Progressive and Nucor all would agree, as each has a very casual dress code. While this may not be an essential ingredient in transforming your organization into a Turbocharged Company, there is certainly ample evidence to suggest that such measures help.

The perks, privileges and status symbols that once separated management from employees are an impediment to Unleashing People Power. They stand out at a time when the efforts of the company must be focused on teamwork—acting as a roadblock to successfully Unleashing People Power. Both from a symbolic and a practical standpoint, ridding your organization of these "luxuries" can only help, not hinder, your efforts to improve your company.

TURBOTIP

Executive "perks" indicate that management is held in higher regard than other employees. This hinders effective communication between management and other employees, causing resentment and discontent.

Share the Gains

When employees achieve an understanding of their company's financial and operating statistics, they are in an excellent position to make positive changes. It has been our observation that most Turbocharged Companies believe in creating incentives for employees, to encourage the search for productivity and other improvements. It is generally recognized that people respond very favorably to the challenges and rewards that incentive plans offer.

The most common incentive program in industry today is profit sharing, whereby employees share in the profits of the corporation. This plan is favored at Southwest Airlines where, in 1994, employees earned over 10 percent of their base salary in profit sharing bonus. While this works very well for some Turbocharged Companies, others have found that this type of plan, by itself, does not achieve all of their objectives. This latter group has found that employees cannot clearly see the connection between productivity and profits. To address this, these Turbocharged Companies have implemented some form of Gainsharing Plan.

A Gainsharing Plan, as its name suggests, shares some of the gain in productivity with employees. Though there are many ways to calculate this, the most common are return on assets, productivity and/or operating efficiency and increase in market share. In practice, you are going to have to determine the appropriate criteria vital to the success of your company. As for payout, in general, we advocate a policy of distributing at least 30 to 40 percent of the value of the gain in productivity to the employees.

One of our clients in the industrial services business was unhappy with the utilization of its equipment. Their trucks and related equipment represented a considerable monetary investment for the firm. To address their concern, we recommended not only focusing on equipment utilization as a daily and weekly goal, but instituting a gainsharing plan based on utilization. As might be expected, equipment utilization improved significantly.

Each Turbocharged Company develops its own unique approach to distributing the gainsharing dollars to employees. Progressive Corporation, for example, bases 60 percent of an individual's gainsharing distribution on the performance of his or her division, while the remaining 40 percent is tied to the overall corporation's performance. Furthermore, within the division, people at various levels can also receive varying percentages of their base pay, based on the market value of their position.

At Nucor, there are four slightly different plans, determined by job function. While, for example, production workers are paid based on production, department managers are paid based on return on assets. Other plans target return on assets and return on shareholders' equity. Mark Clark, who operates a pot on the Crawfordsville, Indiana galvanizing line, points out one of the many advantages of Nucor's productivity plan, "Because people know they can't earn bonuses when the machines are down, everyone chips in to repair and maintain the equipment. As a result, we need a lot less maintenance people, and the machines are up and running a majority of the time."

Finally, at SIFCO Forge Group, all employees, be they production worker, secretary or corporate manager, get the same dollar distribution. This is done to foster total team spirit, and it works.

It is evident by the successes of these companies that the standardization of gainsharing plans serves no valid purpose. What is important is that the plan, whatever it be, is an incentive and motivates employees towards helping the company meet or exceed its goals.

To be truly effective, all Gainsharing Plans will require a periodic "raising of the bar." This is best done by establishing a measure for a base period *(Period 1)*. Then, during Period 2, performance is measured against Period 1. The improvement of Period 2 over Period 1 is the basis for the Gainsharing Award. Moving forward, the productivity during Period 3 is then measured to a new base period *(Period 2)*. This ensures continual improvement—a necessary ingredient in a Turbocharged Company. As it is more difficult to attain each "raised bar," it is important that the percentage of shared gains increase accordingly. This is not only fair, but lets employees know that the company recognizes the additional effort that will be required—and will reward them accordingly. So, for example, if a company paid 30 percent of a gain prior to raising the bar, it might increase the share to 32 or 34 percent after the "bar" has been raised.

You might think that somewhere, there must be a limit to the amount of gains that can be achieved in a company. *If* that happens, it would no longer be appropriate to continue raising the bar. Our experience, however, has demonstrated that the ingenuity of employees in a Turbocharged Company environment will continue to amaze you. You will not believe how far that bar can be raised!

We should mention two important things. First, the periods should be of sufficient duration to allow employees time to achieve, and then surpass, the base period standard. Remember, the objective here is to raise productivity, not save money.

Second, raise the bar in increments that are sufficiently challenging, though not impossible. Having a rationale for the goal helps as well. One such rationale might be, "When you hit this level of productivity, we will reach break-even (where we neither make nor lose money)." The goal may be lofty, but the employees understand why it is there, and what it means. Gainsharing Plans, properly designed, work wonders.

As a final note, be aware that the initial distribution from any gainsharing plan could be significant. Instead of being concerned about this, the company should rejoice in the fact that its employees have embraced this concept. As they continue to earn Gainsharing Awards, productivity—hence profits—will increase as well. Everyone comes out ahead in a Gainsharing Plan.

Incentives, be they profit-sharing or Gainsharing Plans, provide additional encouragement for employees to look beyond the status quo to find ways to lower costs and increase productivity. The company and the employees all benefit from the results of such programs.

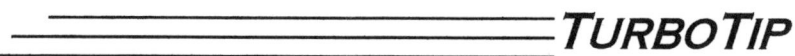
TURBOTIP

One of the best investments a business can ever make is to share the value of improvement with those who made that improvement happen.

Provide Opportunities for Advancement

People are not machines that can be installed in a job and left unchanged for the next 30 years. In today's environment, not only will the technology have changed dramatically, but generally speaking, most employees simply will not stay that long. Employees are no different from management—they are hungry to learn, to advance, to do something different. If they cannot find these opportunities at your company, they will move to another.

When an employee goes to work for a company, both the company and the employee make an investment that can and should pay rich benefits. The company is investing time in recruiting, screening, interviewing, hiring and training the employee. The employee invests not only time in receiving the training, but also in learning how the company works, its strengths and weaknesses. All employees bring to the job their knowledge from previous jobs and academic experience, plus the unlimited potential of their creative ideas. This investment has a significant price tag, of which many companies either are not aware, or simply ignore. The typical Command and Control manager's attitude of "If you don't like it, leave!" can cost the company dearly, for in that circumstance, not only will the organization lose the investment in that one employee, it will then have to start the entire hiring process, with associated expenses, all over again.

Turbocharged Companies realize not only the investment made in the employee, but the untapped potential each brings to the job every day. They tap into this by providing opportunities to advance within the organization. Career-pathing is the technical name for this process. We prefer to view it as continuing a winning combination—your fellow employees and your company.

At Progressive, for example, all jobs are posted internally for two weeks. Any employee can apply for any job. The company's bias toward letting employees advance is seen as an important part of working there. Chuck Chokel, Progressive's Chief Financial Officer, states, "You're not pegged into a slot. I started out in finance, moved to sales, and then product management before coming back to finance. There are no pre-set rules." It has been our experience that Turbocharged Companies allow employees to go as far in the organization as their interest and abilities will take them.

Bryant Scott started at Home Depot as a "Lot Associate"—the person who loads customers' cars and retrieves shopping carts from the parking lot. Today, through hard work and a belief by the company that people can advance through the organization, he is the President of Home Depot's Expo Division. And this is but one of the countless "grow from within" success stories this specialist retailing powerhouse could mention. As Kerrie Flanagan, Vice President of Merchandise Payables at Home Depot puts it, "When you go into our stores and talk with a store manager who has worked his way up to that position, you'll find he can talk to you about finances, purchasing, inventory, or building a store. We build business people."

When employees see that not only are there opportunities to advance within the organization, but that the company will help them attain the skills necessary to make that advancement, their attitudes will change. This help can range anywhere from informal training sessions on a different machine, a PC or a different position, to formal classes conducted both inside and outside the company. It is help that is designed around the employee's skills, experience and desire to grow, focused on assisting the employee to achieve what he or she wants. Notice we say what the *employee* wants—not what management wants. Your punch press operator may want to work in telemarketing. If your training focuses on running a milling machine, where you need help, this training is of little value to her. She will not be motivated to learn, or perform to her capacity.

Most employees function better in an environment that will help them grow. As a result, people are usually willing to work harder today in order to reap rewards tomorrow. To be sure, not everyone feels this way. A small minority of employees, for whatever reason, are presently content to stay where they are. They do not want more responsibility. They do not want to leave their area of comfort and expertise. Turbocharged Companies recognize this and assure the employee that this is okay. This employee can still make many valuable contributions to the organization by being the "rock" in the department.

With the Relentless Pursuit of Productivity and a reduction in management layers, less opportunities will exist within the organization for people to grow. Turbocharged Companies answer this need by directing their efforts at growing significantly, thus allowing their talented people the chance to grow as well.

In a Turbocharged Company, Unleashing People Power means listening to every individual, and helping each advance themselves and progress towards their own career goals

TURBOTIP

The *pain* of today's hard work will become a pleasure—if those efforts lead to the *rewards* of tomorrow.

Treat Employees Fairly and Consistently

Other essential ingredients for Unleashing People Power are fair and consistent treatment and reasonable working conditions. Included in this is reasonable, though not necessarily generous, remuneration. If employees feel that they are not being treated fairly or consistently, they are unlikely to go the extra mile for the company. Fair and consistent treatment of employees includes areas like benefits, working conditions and holidays.

When we started working with SIFCO, they paid manufacturing workers different hourly rates for work on various machines. If a worker was operating a machine that paid a high rate and was then switched to one paying a lower rate, he would receive the lower rate for the time spent operating the second machine. While this strategy made imminent sense to the accounting department, the workers viewed it as unfair. As a result, they would drag out their time on the first machine to delay the pay reduction that came with the second machine. When this company committed itself to Unleashing People Power as part of its goal to become a Turbocharged Company, this policy was abandoned, resulting in an increase in employee morale, and productivity, which more than offset the nominal increase in payroll cost.

Contrary to popular perception, excessively generous remuneration does not, as a rule, achieve high employee morale. A survey conducted by Robert Half International Inc. confirmed that "praise and recognition" (48 percent) and "opportunity for advancement" (27 percent) were considered to be significantly more relevant to employee motivation than "financial compensation" (6 percent).[18]

If people are treated fairly and with respect, and if they are given reasonable opportunity for advancement, they will be satisfied with fair and proper remuneration. If the organization does not provide employees with these basics, however, then overpaying them may be the only way to retain employees. And while the bodies will be there, missing will be the ideas, productivity and "ownership" so vibrantly displayed in Turbocharged Companies.

Money by itself is not a strong motivator. Yet when people, treated fairly and consistently, are given the opportunity to earn additional compensation through a Gainsharing Plan, their motivation is usually enhanced substantially.

When employees are treated fairly and consistently, the company is treating them as partners. It is demonstrating "one for all and all for one." Management is demonstrating with its actions that things are now different in the organization—Command and Control is dead and Unleashed People Power is the wave of the future.

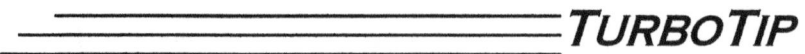

TURBOTIP

Employees cannot enthusiastically commit to an organization if they feel they are being treated unfairly or inconsistently.

Be Sensitive to Employee Insecurity

In today's competitive environment, employee layoffs, company mergers, bankruptcies and even closures seem to be the order of the day. It was not all that long ago when people wanted to work for large corporations because of the job security they seemingly offered. In fact, as recently as the early 1990s, IBM touted its full-employment practice, where layoffs simply did not happen.[19] IBM, and others like it, failed to notice that business conditions had changed dramatically. Virtually no company today can guarantee long-term job security. And employees know it.

Being an employee can be a very insecure experience. Consider the following. American businesses cut over 516,000 jobs during 1994 despite an 11 percent overall increase in corporate profits that year and the 13 percent increase in 1993. The number of jobs cut is higher than the 316,000 that were cut in the recessionary year of 1990, and almost as many as were cut during 1991 when a total of 555,000 jobs were lost.[20] In the face of this, the Command and Control manager's cry of "Just do your job and let me worry about the rest" is as comforting as an Alfred Hitchcock thriller.

Employees who assumed that the layoffs would stop when profitable times returned had a rude awakening. Companies argue that layoffs, despite corporate profitability, are a necessary part of business today. As consumer demand for more value increases, companies are forced to search for ways to increase productivity—and the results are usually job cuts. "No one feels secure," states Peter B. Lewis, CEO of Progressive Corporation. "Insecurity is a fact of life today."

Even if a company is not laying people off, employees have become quite adept at gauging their company's chances for survival, as well as their own. If they see or perceive the company ignoring the realities of the marketplace, additional insecurity will set in. However, when workers see the company taking steps to transform itself into an organization equipped to survive and thrive in the 1990s and beyond, they will have much more confidence in the company's future.

With the erosion of employee security, all businesses have lost an important asset. Instead of focusing all of their energies on their jobs, insecure workers spend a good portion of their time thinking about what they would do if they lost their jobs. To provide a safety blanket, for example, many employees start a part-time business. This results in a substantial amount of their work day and mental energy being diverted from your company. Instead, it is devoted to enhancing this new enterprise—just in case. Other employees may spend time ensuring that their resumes are up-to-date. While most might not actively search for another job, they might send off a resume or two in response to some intriguing want ads. Whether the layoffs are announced or assumed, time spent talking about it in the hallways increases. And as this chatter increases, time and attention to their real job decreases.

Even if employees see the changes being made at the company as positive, insecurity can still be present. "Will I be a part of this new organization?" is forefront in their minds. This worry can sometimes be as crippling to an organization as making no changes. It can have far-reaching effects, even in your teams, as members vie over "who will be left."

All this insecurity leads to a loss of productivity and commitment. In fact, a recent survey of 100 major Chicago area companies listed revitalizing the workforce as the top priority of Human Resource Directors.[21] Employees insecure about their jobs often ask themselves questions like: "Why work hard for an organization that won't be here tomorrow?" "I'm not sure I'll have a job at the end of the week, so why should I care?" "Why help find ways to do things better or more efficiently? I'll probably work myself out of a job." While these often can be self-fulfilling prophecies, they remain the reality of this mindset. As Progressive's Peter Lewis phrases it, "People who worry about getting fired are usually the ones who end up being fired."

So, in all this insecurity, how can the organization get its employees to be as productive, innovative and challenged as it needs them to be? How does a company Unleash People Power when its employees are worried about losing their livelihood? Isn't this a classic Catch 22?

We have found that Turbocharged Companies have two common denominators when it comes to combating employee insecurity—and the loss of productivity it brings. Those common threads are communication that is open, honest and consistent in combination with Unleashing People Power. Let's review each of these.

Combating employee insecurity starts with good communication. When a company is totally honest and open with its employees, whether the news is good or bad, the employees will begin to trust the company. Development of this trust is vital to the Turbocharged Company Process. They will stop worrying about when "the other shoe will fall" because management has been very open with them. After all, they can see that order count is slipping. Telling people that "sales just had a bad couple of weeks" is sticking your head in the sand—and employees know it. On the other hand, telling them nothing is even worse.

Human beings thirst for information. When we see a situation developing, we need information so we know how to act—and react. This reflex is instinctive. It probably goes back to the days of the cave dwellers when, on hearing a rustle in the bushes, early man needed information—to know if he should run away from a predator, or greet a friend. So this information vacuum needs to be filled. If the company's leaders provide information that is clear and honest, this need will be satisfied. Then the employee can honestly assess the situation and take actions that are appropriate. When no other information is forthcoming, however, the employee will fill this information vacuum using whatever data is known, can be presumed or can be gleaned from the rumor mill. This latter information is always pessimistic, for by nature we prepare for the worst. It is at this point that true paranoia sets in, diverting valuable energy from productivity to anxiety.

Instead, employees should be told the truth—that sales are down, management is not sure why and if this trend continues, layoffs might have to be considered. Yes, employees will worry and become somewhat insecure—but remember, we said there were two parts to this solution.

The second part is Unleashing People Power—when employees are given a degree of influence over the company, and its destiny. Unleashing People Power gives employees influence, but also responsibility. In the situation we have described, traditional Command and Control employees would sit and worry, powerless to do anything about the situation. But as Unleashed Employees, their initial insecurity will turn naturally toward a "What are we going to do about this?" attitude. The Customer team finds out what the problems in the marketplace are, and how to enhance customer satisfaction. The Productivity team reviews where savings in purchasing, inventory and other areas can be made. The Production team figures out how to give the customer what he or she wants, and at a lower cost. The list goes on. Insecurity gives way to positive action.

The difference between apathy and action is straightforward communication and People Power. No, it's not a miracle cure— but it is pretty close! Southwest Airlines' employees could have agreed that cutting the route schedule was the only way for the company to survive back in the early days. Instead, they found a way to operate the airline with 25 percent less planes. SIFCO could have closed its plant; instead, it told the employees what the problems were and gave them the latitude to solve them. Yes, employees felt insecure, but they channeled those insecurities into finding solutions, instead of worrying.

Communication + People Power—it's a very powerful combination. It can overcome the basic insecurity most employees feel about their jobs in today's environment. And it turns problems and worries into energized employees, willing to do whatever it takes to secure the company's future—and their own.

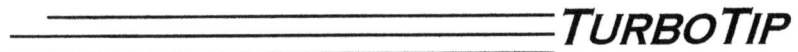

TURBOTIP

Employees who are confident that their company is working toward an excellent future will not need to devote any significant time to developing "fall-back" positions, in case they lose their jobs.

Seek Round Pegs for Round Holes

While we have repeatedly witnessed ordinary people achieving extraordinary results in a team environment, the effectiveness of any team can be compromised if it has the wrong players. As Tiona Thompson, Chief of Human Resources at Progressive Insurance states it, "If the people chemistry on a team isn't right, it doesn't matter how good the players are. It will never work. It is important for team leaders to realize when this situation arises and take the steps necessary to correct the situation."

Chemistry between team members is one factor—personality traits are another. By the time we have reached adulthood, our personalities have pretty much been formed. Perhaps we are extroverts, perhaps introverts. We may be logical thinkers, weighing each bit of information carefully in order to make a decision. Or we may be instinctive decision makers. The list goes on. While we may be able to step outside ourselves and temporarily take on a new personality, we generally are not comfortable doing so. We will return to our "real self" as quickly as we can.

From our own experiences and observations, we found it is vitally important to match the person with the job. There are salespeople, for example, who are excellent cold-callers. Others are much better at servicing a customer, building a long-term relationship. It is obvious that the latter is the person you want to handle your 10 best customers. The first should be assigned to search for new accounts.

Unquestionably, the factors that most distinguish Turbocharged Companies are the quality and effectiveness of their people. We have seen over and over that companies that outperform their competitors in hiring, training and motivating their employees enjoy a significant advantage. Turbocharged Companies take extra steps to ensure that the person they are hiring not only fits well in the job, but also with the company. They often rely on tools like team interviews, where some members of the work team take turns interviewing potential candidates. Candidates are often impressed at how well prepared team members are during these interviews, and at the type of in-depth questions that are asked.

This approach, while seemingly radical, ensures there is a good "fit" between a potential candidate and members of the team. In our experience, this has proven invaluable in keeping the synergy of a team in place.

The Home Depot considers employee selection and training key to its success. Don Singletary, Home Depot's Vice President of Employee Relations, explains it this way, "We start by trying to hire the right kind of people—people who have the same values, who want to take care of the customer, who are entrepreneurs. Then we tell these new employees to forget almost everything they learned from other retailers. We teach them to be good listeners. We have them go through a one-week orientation program where employees get to hear (from founders Bernard Marcus and Arthur Blank) the history of the company, why we exist and how we want the customer to be treated." With friendly people who have been trained on the products in the store, customers feel much more confident about their purchases. They are happy, and return again, and Home Depot continues to grow.[22]

The vast majority of Nucor's 5,900 employees are production workers, engaged in making steel. Yet Larry A. Roos, Vice President and General Manager of the firm's very successful

Crawfordsville, Indiana plant, states, "We invest a lot of time in hiring the right people. We like to hire positive, team players. We put all our people through an intensive psychological and interview hiring process. And we don't delegate this to the Personnel Department, either. Each supervisor does his own hiring."

Other tools to improve hiring include various personality profiles. The Myers-Briggs Personality Profile is an excellent tool in the hands of a trained interpreter and counselor of results. Other excellent tools are the Personal Profile System by Performax Systems, Organizational Analysis and Design by OAD, Inc., and Personal Style Interview by Doctors R. Craig Hogan and David W. Champagne. Still other profiles are available in a software format designed to run on a PC like Brooks Mitchell's Computerized Employee Selection from Aspen Tree Software. Such electronic tests provide faster, though more stylized, hiring information. We must be sure to note, however, that any such test should be weighed against the impressions gained during the interview process, as well as from thorough reference checks.

We do not advocate hiring only in the likeness and mindset of everyone else on the team. That would lead to restraint on creativity and ingenuity. Instead, we recommend avoiding hiring candidates who possess obvious personality traits that make the person unsuitable for the position or the company. For example, Southwest Airlines tries to hire people who like to have fun—and this applies to all positions within the company. Overly serious people do not do well at Southwest, and very few make it past the initial screening. Others, (like MBNA, an extremely successful financial institution based in Delaware) look for people who like other people. They have found that people who genuinely like other people treat customers better and make the company more successful.[23] Obviously, a loner would not fit into this environment.

Good hiring decisions rank as one of the most important determinants in the ability to Unleash People Power in an organization—and in the ultimate success of the business. Because of this, it is essential to devote a significant amount of time to this process. If you view each hire as a long-term relationship, taking a few extra days or weeks to get the right candidate up-front will pay off in the long run.

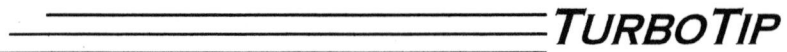

TURBOTIP

No matter how long it takes to find people who are well suited and qualified for the job, the effort will be far less costly, painful and time consuming than having to replace someone who does not fit in with the organization.

Watch Those Changes . . .

"Times change, and we change with them too"

— OWEN's Epigrammata (1615)

In these times of rapidly changing technology, customer expectations and competition, it is rare that a company can be doing the exact same thing today that it did 10 years ago. While this is true, as humans we still resist change. Jack Welch, CEO of GE, puts it this way, "Change has no constituency. People like the status quo. They like the way it was."[24]

When you make changes in your organization, we encourage you to think those changes over very carefully. Being open to change is vital to any organization. However, management must be careful to implement change judiciously. Recognizing the difficulties people have with change, it should only happen if it is necessary for the success of the company. Important changes must be differentiated from *whims*. For change to be effective, all employees must understand the need for, and rationale behind, the change. If, after appropriate explanation, employees feel the changes are *necessary* for the success of the company, they will support them. If, however, they see them as just another in a series of missteps, false starts or "wild-goose-chases," employees will resist the changes.

When you decide a change is necessary, plan each strategy and each step with as much diligence as possible, then stay the course.

Yes, you will have to make minor adjustments along the way. But these adjustments should be within the basic framework of the change you have charted.

While change is inevitable, it takes time to implement. Some authorities believe it takes six months to fully implement and embrace a massive organizational change. If the company is constantly changing direction, people will never catch up. They will give up, and basically wait for the organization to make up its mind.

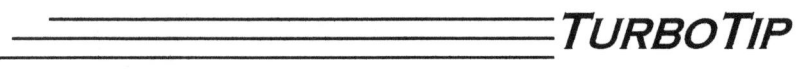

Too many zigs and zags will take even the most dedicated mission off course. Chart your course carefully and stick with it.

Give Something Back

A trait we have noticed in the great majority of Turbocharged Companies, though certainly not a prerequisite, is the company's desire to give something back to the community. At Southwest Airlines, the Ronald McDonald House[i] is the focus of its corporate charitable program. In addition, employees generously donate their time to various local charity events. In 1995, Home Depot will contribute over $8 million in building materials and cash grants, plus volunteer support to larger charities, including Habitat for Humanity and Christmas in April, as well as local community projects.

Beyond tax write-offs and any other "gain" from such activities, many Turbocharged Companies feel a sense of responsibility for the communities in which they work. "We give," states Southwest's Herb Kelleher, "not because we have to, but because we want to." Home Depot's Bernie Marcus states, "In addition to making money and rewarding our stockholders, we are doing many things in the local communities. I am so proud of this company. Everybody in the company is involved in giving back to the community, and I think that has helped make the culture of the company a lot more meaningful."[25]

By being charitable with their time as well as money, these companies achieve a twofold objective. They make a genuine and sincere contribution to the welfare of their communities. Further,

---

[i] Ronald McDonald House is a service mark of McDonald's Corporation

they also stimulate a culture that encourages a "giving" spirit, which creates an environment wherein employees are more likely to be "giving" (courteous, considerate) to their customers.

At Nucor, the slant is a little different. Ken Iverson, the company's Chairman, explains it this way, "We believe that charity begins at home. While we support traditional charities at the local plant level, our corporate "giving back" program focuses on our employees." Nucor provides $2,000 per year for four years of college for every child of every employee. John Correnti, Nucor's President, relates a very interesting conversation one of his plant managers had with an employee when the program was just being announced.

> *"Do I understand correctly—the company is going to offer some scholarships?" one employee asked. "Yeah" the manager replied, not sure where the conversation was headed. "Well, I'd sure like to get my kids some," said the employee. The manager was taken aback by the employee's comment and replied, "Well, we're going to give it to everyone." The employee fired back, "What do you mean everybody? Do you mean all my kids are going to receive it? I have 11 children!" The manager responded, "Yes, as long as you work here, all your children will receive it." "Work here?" the employee shouted. "There's no way you could drive me away!"*

Every company handles this type of program differently. As we noted, while it is not a requirement to becoming a Turbocharged Company, we do pass it along as a refreshing characteristic that most have in common.

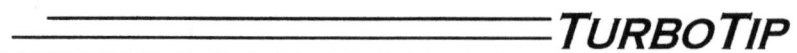

TURBOTIP

The rewards that companies and their employees experience when lending a helping hand in their communities are not only measured in dollars and cents.

The Lessons of Unleashing People Power

Unleashing People Power is the critical First Foundation on which the other Foundations of a Turbocharged Company are built. In order to Unleash the secret weapon of People Power, it is essential to:

Provide employees information—About the company's goals and progress toward those goals.

Develop an open culture—Abandon traditional management practices that stifle creativity and enthusiasm, treat employees with respect, and involve employees—as individuals and in teams—in planning and decision making.

Create incentives—Reward employees who energetically search for ways to do things better.

Be sensitive—Always consider employees' need to advance themselves; the insecurity of corporate life; and the problems resulting from frequent changes in direction.

Exercise patience and diligence—Select employees who are well suited to the tasks asked of them.

Foundation Two—REVERE YOUR CUSTOMERS

THE
TURBOCHARGED COMPANY
PROCESS

UNLEASH PEOPLE POWER

REVERE CUSTOMERS   RELENTLESSLY PURSUE PRODUCTIVITY

DOMINATE MICRONICHE

OUTPERFORM COMPETITORS

SUPERIOR RETURNS ON SHAREHOLDERS' EQUITY

Once People Power has been Unleashed, you and your fellow employees can begin focusing on Revering Customers—treating customers with the utmost respect, and placing their satisfaction as your company's highest priority. You will see that determining the customer's needs, and then structuring your organization to exceed those needs, is the key to long-term success. Achieve this, and your customers will want to do business with you.

Look at Your Customers a Little Differently

"We are not in the automotive business, we're in the business of satisfying customers."

— Robert J. Eaton, Chairman & CEO, Chrysler Corporation

Not all that long ago, a customer walking into an automobile dealership brought out the "killer instinct" in car salespeople. To the salesperson, the customer was there to be defeated—to be sold a car before he or she had a chance to escape. The focus was on making as much money on each transaction as possible. There was little concern for repeat customer business—just making the sale today.

Saturn changed all that for domestic dealerships. The one-price, no-haggle approach to selling cars took a skeptical public by surprise. If that wasn't enough, the tour through the service department and introductions to service technicians, office managers and sales managers certainly went a long way toward proving Saturn had nothing to hide. From those first steps, the entire approach to selling automobiles has changed. At Chrysler, it is called the Customer One concept. Translated, Chrysler's approach is not only to serve the customer, it is to delight him or her. Courtesy and respect are not the goals—they are imperative! The order of the day is world-class treatment for people who purchase Chrysler products. Chrysler has backed that commitment with a program designed to retrain dealership personnel in the Customer One concept.[26]

The major change in thinking in Detroit, and in many areas of American business, is that the customer is not the enemy. The customer is not one to be fooled, conquered or "sold." Those words denote a one-sided, self-serving approach to business. Instead, Turbocharged Companies have found that treating the customer as an asset and a friend, is a far more healthy and beneficial basis on which to build a business relationship.

Turbocharged Companies go out of their way to Revere Their Customers. They are not pushing a product; instead, they are listening to their customers' needs and responding appropriately. Their people do not say "that's not my job" when a customer calls, but find a way to solve the customer's problem or request.

At Home Depot, employees will do whatever it takes to satisfy a customer, including taking back product from a competitor. By providing such service, Home Depot is confident that the next time the customer needs something from a home improvement center, he or she will remember the service received at Home Depot and shop there. It is a philosophy that seems to be working quite well for this retailer.

Today's Turbocharged Companies know that the customer is the reason for their existence, not an outlet for their manufacturing capacity. They realize that it is far more financially advantageous to keep a customer than it is to find a new one.

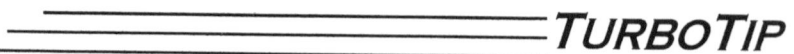 *TURBOTIP*

Focus on what customers need, rather than what your company has to sell.

Eliminate the "Sales" Department!

We frequent a little restaurant that treats its customers like royalty. It starts as we enter the front door. While there is an official hostess, if she is busy, someone else seats us. It might be a waitress. It might be the owner. But no customer is left standing for more than a few seconds. The service is prompt, the food well prepared—though not anything fancy—and the prices reasonable. Our cup never runs dry—the staff always makes sure it's full of fresh, hot coffee. If we need anything, anyone who works there will get it. There is no, "I'll get your waiter for you." If we are in a hurry, and tell them, they will make sure we are out at the designated time. If we order something that will take too much time to prepare, they will tell us and suggest an alternative that is quicker to prepare. We have an enjoyable dining experience each time we go there. Others must enjoy the same service—the restaurant is always packed.

We have all been in restaurants where the experience is considerably less than this—where you wait for five minutes for the hostess to seat you, as three other employees stand idly by. Where asking for a refill on your coffee makes you feel like you are robbing the place. Where no one can help you except the waiter or waitress assigned to your table. Such restaurants make the dining experience anything but pleasurable. You certainly do not want to return anytime in the near future.

The difference in those experiences is one of philosophy. Traditional restaurants are in the business of making and serving food to make money. Everyone has a job, and does only that. The customer is a necessary evil that wants too much, eats too slowly and leaves too little tip. Our little restaurant is different. It is in business to provide a wonderful dining experience. To do this, they make and serve food. If the customer has had a pleasant dining experience, the bill will be paid. That customer will tell others, who will come, dine and enjoy themselves. The cycle goes on, and so will the profits. The difference is the focus. In our restaurant, everyone goes out of his or her way to ensure you have that enjoyable dining experience. In other restaurants, little attention is paid to the dining experience, just "What did they order?" "When will they finish so we can fill the table again?" and "Did they leave a large enough tip?" We ask you, which restaurant will still be around five years from now, as busy as ever, and which will be ready to close?

Consider the door-to-door encyclopedia salesperson. He or she starts off with a quota for the day. Twenty sets have to be sold by the end of the day. It does not matter if you want, or even need, the set; the salesperson's goal is to get you to buy it. Buying, selling, cash registers ringing—those are the important marks of a "sales" person. "Move the product" because we are making more and need the room. How much profit did we make? Customer satisfaction is translated to mean "Is the customer satisfied enough so he/she will not complain or worse yet, return the product?"

Telemarketers are often guilty of imposing themselves on potential customers with the sole objective of "making the sale." It is the rare person who has not undergone the unwelcome hounding by persistent telephone salespeople, hawking anything from dry basements to stocks and bonds. Even if you try to terminate the conversation politely with a sincere, "I'm sorry, you've caught me at a bad moment," the sales pitch goes on and on. "I know you're busy, I just wanted to tell you about . . ." they respond. By this time your anger has taken control—you terminate the call shortly or slam the phone down in an abrupt disconnect. Such salespeople are not sensitive to the needs or wants of the customer. Their only concern is the sale. To achieve this, they are willing to antagonize 95 or more people out of 100 to get five who will listen to their sales pitch. This is a classic "make the sale at all costs" approach, with little regard for the customer.

Turbocharged Companies operate differently. They exist to serve the needs of their customers. Instead of forcing products or services, inappropriate or not, onto the marketplace, they produce solutions to satisfy their customers' needs.

In Turbocharged Companies, there is no "sales" department, per se. While they may have a department with this name, the company's ultimate goal is customer satisfaction. The greatest example of this is Southwest Airlines, where Colleen Barrett's title is not Executive Vice President of Sales, but Executive Vice President of Customers. Southwest's focus on the customer is underscored by not only how they treat their customers, but how they are structured as well. There is no "sales" department at Southwest!

While "sales" is the lifeblood of any business, Turbocharged Companies realize that "sales" are the result of properly serving the needs of customers. Moreover, they realize that customer satisfaction, and its resultant byproduct "sales," is not the sole responsibility of a department named sales. Every employee is ultimately responsible for customer satisfaction, and hence sales.

That concept is no better illustrated than by again looking at General Motor's Saturn Division. At Saturn, when you decide to purchase a car, you are taken on a tour of the dealership. As we mentioned, you are introduced to the service people who will keep your car in repair, the parts people who will get whatever replacement parts you need, even the receptionist, who answers the phone when you call. You soon realize there is more to buying this car than a salesperson's empty promises. There is an entire customer service team behind you. When you pick up your new car, a team gathers around you. They let out a cheer, take your picture, and hand you your keys.[27] What an experience!

Customers do not always have to be external, either. Co-workers are customers as well. Every day, each of us relies on others to help us do our jobs, just as others rely on us to help them do theirs. **Turbocharged Companies place significant emphasis on treating internal customers with as much care and concern as external ones.** A happy internal work force makes external work proceed all that much smoother, which manifests itself in improved customer relations. Part of Southwest's Mission Statement sums it up best: "Above all, employees will be provided with the same concern, respect and caring attitude within the organization that they are expected to share externally with every Southwest Customer."

In Turbocharged Companies, there is no "selling" department. Every employee is responsible for meeting the needs of the customer—both internal and external. Doing this, along with implementing the other Foundations of a Turbocharged Company, will put your organization in a much better position to enjoy the profits from its labors. Are you ready to "eliminate" your Sales Department?

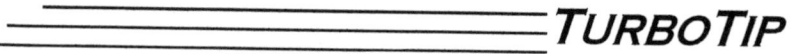 *TURBOTIP*

Every employee of a business has a role and responsibility in satisfying customers—be they internal or external.

Ensure Customer Satisfaction

"It's no secret that we've grown dramatically in the last few years. And we did it by listening and responding to our customers."

— Grace Nichols, President, Victoria's Secret[28]

Turbocharged Companies make sure their customers are satisfied, no matter what it takes. They realize that, in the long run, only satisfied customers return. Contrast our pleasant little restaurant experience mentioned previously with this one—

You go out to dinner at a very popular restaurant. You have enjoyed several very fine meals at this restaurant and are looking forward to eating there. Feeling a little adventurous, you have ordered something you have never had before, but sounds enticing. When the meal arrives, you take a mouthful, only to be very put-off by the taste. It is not that it is bad—just not to your liking—certainly not anything you want to finish.

You call the server over and explain the situation. A few minutes later the manager appears. She advises that she has tasted a similar meal in the kitchen, and that it is just fine. You acknowledge that it may be cooked perfectly—it is just not to your liking. The long and short of it is that the manager refuses to do anything about the situation. She feels she lived up to her end of the agreement—her staff provided what you ordered. Not wanting to finish a meal you do not like, you get up, pay the bill and leave.

How many companies do you know that do the very same thing? "I'm sorry the slacks don't fit, sir, but you purchased them and wore them, now they're yours." Yes, the integrity of today's profit was maintained. But in the long term, will you go back to that restaurant or clothing store again? Doubtful. Studies have shown it is more likely that you will tell 11 of your friends about the terrible experience you had. They will tell their friends or business acquaintances. Pretty soon, the business has fewer and fewer customers.

To make matters tougher, satisfaction with a product or service is subjective. It can only be measured by the recipient of the product or service. The provider is presumptuous at best if he/she believes that judgment can be made for the recipient. Earnie Deavenport, Jr., Chairman and CEO of Eastman Chemical Company, puts it this way, "One thing became very clear to me early in my career. What I was working on would not be a quality product until the customer said it was a quality product. My company does not define quality—our customers define quality." Francois Castaing, Vice President of Engineering at Chrysler, states, "If you do not try to get back to satisfying the customer, who is becoming more and more demanding, every day, you begin to lose ground."[29] The old thought of "If I lose this customer, I'll simply go out and get another one" has to be replaced, as the cost of doing business this way continues to mount. Satisfying the customer in the first place winds up being the lowest cost, highest return way to do business.

As we travel across the country, we have seen an interesting development in many motels and hotels. An increasing number of these facilities have signs in their lobby, and in the individual guest rooms, that proclaim "Your stay with us will be enjoyable, or you don't pay." Here, the innkeeper has placed customer satisfaction ahead of occupancy rates and the bottom line. The innkeeper knows that satisfied guests are more likely to dine in his restaurant, visit his gift shop and order in-room movies than an unsatisfied guest. The focus of that innkeeper and his staff is making your stay a pleasurable one; everything else is a result of that attitude, not the goal.

When Saturn announced its first ever product recall, skeptics could not believe it. The problem had only occurred in 34 cars out of 352,833 cars sold. By government standards, it was insignificant. A government-mandated recall had never even been discussed.[30] Still, Saturn was adamant. They would not only recall each of those cars, they would make the repair as painless as possible for Saturn owners. Service departments extended their hours and put extra people on to handle the problem. Some dealers pitched tents, offering balloons, barbecued food or coffee and doughnuts to Saturn owners as they waited for the 30-minute repair to be completed.[31] To conduct the recall, Saturn spent every penny of the profit it had finally just earned. Management felt "that was the Saturn way."

Sometimes underscoring the importance of a customer takes different forms. SIFCO Forge Group had a policy of issuing white hard hats to all visitors to the plant. This included suppliers, auditors, service people, contractors and customers. Because the white hats were issued universally to anyone who was not an employee, little attention was paid to people wearing them. They did not know if the individual was a customer—or a sales rep, there to sell more shop towels. Once People Power had been Unleashed in this organization, a change was made. Some of the white hats were painted yellow—and only issued to customers. Then, as Manufacturing Team Leader Mike Candow relates, "When a yellow hard hat is spotted, the employees know it is a customer—the person funding their pay checks." The employees' attitudes changed, the customers sensed it, and it gave them a better feeling about doing business with the company.

Revering the Customer means providing the goods or services the consumer wants—to the complete satisfaction of the consumer. This policy puts your "money where your mouth is" when it comes to customer service. It will not only make believers out of your customers, it will bring them back again and again.

TURBOTIP

A business has not honored its contract with a customer until the customer is satisfied—and only the customer can determine when this has happened.

Meeting Customer Expectations Isn't Good Enough!

When Disneyland in California was being built, the accountants, engineers and construction people had decided that the Fantasyland Castle would be constructed last. Walt Disney heard of this and immediately called together those who had made the decision. From a work flow and economic standpoint, it just made sense, they explained. Walt would have none of that. "I want everyone working on the project to see that castle all day and every day, so they don't forget what it is we're trying to do here," he explained. Walt wanted his guests to step outside the cares of the everyday world for a few hours and just be able to enjoy themselves. Fantasyland Castle represented the great white castle in all our dreams. The trades people weren't just constructing an amusement park—they were constructing an experience, and Walt didn't want them to forget it.[32]

What Walt Disney knew better than anyone else in his field was to go for the "wow" factor. A nice amusement park, filled with more traditional attractions, would have brought customers. Walt wanted to go further. He wanted to provide an environment where people would not only come once or twice, but over and over again. He wanted to give them much more than they expected. And he did this not only in buildings and attractions, but in the way guests were treated. Disney does not have a Customer Service Department—they do not even have customers! But they do have a Guest Relations Department to handle all the needs of each guest, individually. The difference is not semantics—it's an experience instead of a ticket price.

When you provide your customers with exactly what they want, that's meeting their needs. And for many companies, that alone will be an important first step. But in order to be a Turbocharged Company, your organization must exceed your customers' expectations.

At Southwest Airlines, exceeding the customer's expectations is expected—employees look for ways to do it. Southwest calls it "Positively Outrageous Service"[i]. Here is one of thousands of examples that could be quoted:

> *During the summer of 1989, Ontario Customer Service Agent Joni Hallmark was working the ticket counter when a customer checked in with his pet. A dog. A big dog. A big, mean dog. Well, the customer wanted to take his dog on vacation. When Joni told him Southwest does not transport animals, fangs began to show—both the man's and the dog's. It seems that the man had to make a connection, using nonrefundable tickets, with another carrier later in his trip. He had to get on his planned flight. As Joni explained it, 'what was this guy to do?'*

> *Joni offered to take the man's dog home and care for it during the entire length of the customer's two-week vacation. Since the man had figured the airline would provide the dog (we'll call him 'Bagtag') with a dog cage, the animal came equipped with only a leash. Consequently, Bagtag spent the rest of the day tied to a baggage cart—a cart no one could go near except Joni.*

---

[i] Based on the book *Positively Outrageous Service*, written by T. Scott Gross. Published by MasterMedia Limited ©1991

Needless to say, everyone was happy when Joni and Bagtag went home at the end of her shift.

For half a month, Joni fed and entertained Bagtag, who repaid her kindness by tearing up the grass in her backyard. The cost of Bagtag's upkeep came directly from Joni's own pocket. At the allotted time, the customer returned, claimed Bagtag, and both went happily on their way. The customer probably never fully realized what Joni had done.

Ken Iverson of Nucor relates a different sort of "wowing" opportunity:

We had steel that we brought in from Poland at one time for our structural joist division. We were asking for a special 50,000 PSI yield strength. The first shipment was just fine, but we needed more steel, so we ordered a second shipment. This shipment came in at only 36,000 PSI yield strength, but we did not find that out until the joists had been made and shipped to a variety of customers.

We had to pay each of our customers to let us go to their jobs, bring the defective joists down, and replace them. The customers were unaware there was any problem until we told them. We could have slipped it through, but that's not our way. You have to be honest with your customers.

Exceeding their customers' expectations is considered standard operating procedure at The Home Depot, as Chairman Bernard Marcus relates it—

We try to treat every customer like they were family. If, for example, your brother-in-law came into the store and said his hot water heater just went out, and for some reason your store was out of water heaters, you would naturally call every other Home Depot store. Once you located one, you would get into your car, go over and get it, and bring it back to your brother-in-law, waiting at the store. If no Home Depot store had the needed heater in stock, you would call each of your competitors until you found one—then would go out, buy it, and bring it back to the store. And that's the way we want you to treat each and every one of our customers.

Finally, noted business author Tom Peters demonstrated his belief in this concept in his latest book, *In Pursuit of WOW,*[i] which outlines the many advantages of providing service levels over and above the customer's expectations. The power of WOW cannot be underestimated.

Turbocharged Companies know that when their customers exclaim "wow" at the product or service they have received, the company will be in a much better position to enjoy repeat business from that customer. The "wow" shows the company cares enough not only to meet expectations, but to go far beyond. This is the "value added" portion of the business. This is the server and the wine steward and the chef at your favorite restaurant who do those little "extras" that put the finishing touch on your dining experience. What it boils down to is this: We enjoy receiving more than we expect; why should our customers be any different?

When you think about it, the trust between a new customer and a sales representative is a fragile thing. When you go out and purchase an automobile, you generally feel quite good about your purchase. You got the car you have dreamed of, outfitted just the way you want it, at a fair price. You drive away with your new purchase, nostrils filled with the aromas only a new car can have, paint sparkling in the sunlight. It is a pretty wonderful feeling. A few weeks later, you notice a few items that need adjusting, and you take the car back for service. Without designating or designing this situation as such, you are putting the dealership to the test. How are they going to handle your car and your adjustments? If the adjustments take a long time, if the service manager is rude, if the adjustments cost you time, inconvenience or money, the "honeymoon" will be over. The company did not stand behind its word—and did not meet your expectations. If,

---

[i] Copyright © 1994 by Excel,/ A California Partnership

however, their service is as convenient and prompt as you were told it was, your confidence will be reinforced. Further, if the dealership washes and waxes your car before you pick it up, they will have exceeded your expectations. They will have gone out of their way to show they care—and you will feel that much better about the organization and the people behind it. If the dealership follows that service call up with a phone call from the sales representative or service manager, it is doubly great. A call just to make sure you're completely satisfied with your purchase and the service you received goes a long, long way toward assuring you that your business is appreciated, and your satisfaction important.

To be sure, the expectations of our customers are continually changing and always increasing. And we must address not only those increased levels of expectations, but even more. Cynthia Fedus, President of Victoria's Secret Catalog Division, puts it this way:

> *"When a business is growing and successful, there is always the temptation to say, 'We've figured it out.' But you can never say that, because the customer is always changing. So we keep trying to figure out new ways to do it better."*[33]

By learning to exceed your customer's expectations, you not only keep them now, you will keep them long-term. You will build valuable customer loyalty—the best resource for enhancing your bottom line. And this will result in gaining the lowest cost, most effective, advertising that there is—word-of-mouth endorsements.

TURBOTIP

Every employee should be constantly on the lookout for opportunities to "wow" the customer.

Create the Maytag Syndrome

No doubt you have seen the Maytag[i] commercials that depict a very lonely old Maytag repairman who has nothing to do. According to the commercials, Maytag washers and dryers (and all the other products they sell) are built so well that they virtually never need to be repaired. If one ever should need repairing, never fear, the commercial states, the old repairman, who has been polishing his tools and re-reading the repair manuals, will jump at the chance to put these skills into actual use.

Aside from being a very clever endorsement of the reliability of Maytag products, the commercial underscores another important quality of Turbocharged Companies—they have time to satisfy the needs of their customers. Not only do they have time, they are anxiously awaiting your call—yet ironically, because everyone is so pleased with their products or services, they get very few calls.

If we were to examine your business today, we would probably find that your organization is already pretty lean. Those employees remaining have had a lot of additional tasks added to their already-burdened work load. These people are so buried in their day-to-day routine, the last thing they need is a customer with a problem. And we will tell you, this is a very dangerous situation to be in. At a time when a customer needs the company the most—a time when the company has the opportunity to exceed the customer's expectations—the company is simply too

---

[i] Maytag is a registered trademark of Maytag Corporation

busy. The day-to-day grind of getting all these tasks done gets in the way of doing what you are in business to do—serve the customer.

Turbocharged Companies are structured so that employees have time for customers. Jobs and workflows are rearranged so that no activities prevent the customer from being satisfied. When the customer has a question or a problem, or just simply needs help, someone is there to respond enthusiastically. There are no telephone busy signals, recorded messages or long lines in which to stand. Having time for the customer is not an additional responsibility, it is the company's first priority. It is not an inconvenience, it is your company's reason for existence. Nothing—not a presidential summons, meetings, paperwork, you name it—must stand in the way of your company's first priority—serving your customers.

The internal processes of your company have to be reviewed to determine better ways to do things. This will enable employees to get their work done in the time left after solving customers' problems. Notice we did not say that reviewing work flows would give employees time to handle customer problems—that is putting the cart before the horse. Instead, reviewing these internal processes, which the customer never sees and could care less about, allows your employees time to do them *after* the needs of the customers are met.

When your company does this—making the customer your number-one priority—imagine the difference this will make. Your customers will call and, instead of talking to someone who is already overburdened, they will talk to an employee whose primary job is satisfying their needs. Imagine the difference it will make in the employee's attitude, tone of voice, helpfulness and time spent on the problem. Imagine how your customer will feel, having called someone whose sole job seems to be the satisfaction of his or her needs. What a refreshing change of pace.

The Maytag Syndrome—waiting for opportunities to be of service—needs to encompass every employee who has contact with customers. In the end, great products and all the best customer service can be destroyed by a receptionist who feels the customer's call is an intrusion in an already busy day—or by the shipping clerk who throws the product in the shipping box with little or no care about the product's condition or appearance.

If everyone who has contact with customers takes the time to ensure the customers are happy and satisfied, those customers will return, and will tell friends and business acquaintances. When your company's actions back up your claims, your customers will notice, and your business will grow. The way to provide this level of customer service is to structure the organization so employees have the time and resources to assist the customer. Procedures, processes and systems that prevent this, or interfere with it, are a roadblock to Revering the Customer and must be modified or removed.

TURBOTIP

Dealing with customers' questions, concerns or problems should be a much sought-after opportunity to create a favorable impression—not an intrusion in a busy schedule.

The Customer Shouldn't Have to Pay!

It is an unfortunate fact of business life today that most businesses subject their customers to inconveniences, delays, errors and frustrations, due solely to the company's inadequacies. In essence, they make their customers pay for their shortcomings.

A furniture rental business had a billing system that worked well for it—but not for its customers. Every time a customer wanted to rent something, a separate invoice would be created. Not bad if the customer rented one or two items, but some customers would rent as many as 30 to 40 items in a month. That meant 30 to 40 separate invoices for every month the items remained out on rent. The customers hated this system and complained bitterly.

This company had persisted in this practice for years. While they would have liked to change, doing so would involve a great deal of computer programming and would involve significant resources (to the tune of several hundred thousand dollars). From the company's point of view, it was a lot of money to spend. While the company was well aware of the complaints of their customers, they did not take decisive action to change the situation.

One of three things could have resulted from this situation. First, nothing. The company could have continued the multiple invoice practice, and the customers would remain bitter. Eventually the customers would drift away to another supplier whose level of paperwork matched their needs and expectations. Second, the customers could have confronted the company and demanded the changes be made, or they would withdraw their business. While this gets the customers what they wanted, it has a very high price in terms of trust and level of comfort. Finally, the company could begin Revering the Customer, and adapt its systems to their needs. Fortunately, the company took this last course of action. To say their customers were pleased would be an understatement.

Turbocharged Companies give the highest priority to meeting customer needs and ensuring customer satisfaction. A customer should never be inconvenienced because a system, designed for internal processing comfort, causes them additional burden. How can you Revere the Customer when you are making him pay for your company's shortfalls?

While the rental company's experience is perhaps a glaring example of inconveniencing the customer, there are less obvious examples. A major retail chain of electronics stores always asks for the customer's name and address prior to ringing up the sale. It does not take a lot of time, but customers always wonder why this information is necessary—especially since their competitors do not require this same information. While we are sure that the store has a valid reason for entering this data into its computer system, the customer sees no direct or indirect benefit from this system. Further, this information does not seem to be used for mailing list purposes, as there are always new catalogs and flyers available at the stores that have not been sent directly to the customer. So in addition to being inconvenient, this system creates more than a bit of suspicion.

It would be so much better if the store did not impose this inconvenience on the customer. At a minimum, the store should explain its policy, *i.e.* security for credit card use, automatic registration of hardware and software purchases, frequent purchaser program. In this way, customers would see a benefit from the system. Imagine—instead of filling out all those silly warranty registration postcards, the store's computer does it for you. Now *that* is Revering Your Customers!

Finally, one client of ours got into the habit of shipping orders ahead of the date requested by the customers. This was done particularly near the end of the month or quarter, when it would improve productivity and shipping goals. While great for the shipping department, the billing folks and the accountants, this system was very inconvenient for the customer. In today's world of just-in-time shipments and careful controls over inventories, customers want shipments when they specify—not when it is convenient for the vendor. Today, it is a problem if shipments arrive early or late. As companies watch their assets more carefully, shipping early—once the sign of a good supplier—is now often considered a detriment and can cost you the customer. Again, your customers should not have to "pay" so that your firm can make its numbers. If you Revere Your Customers—if their needs come first—then everything else will fall into place. A just-in-time delivery means just that . . . not earlier and not later.

Turbocharged Companies are continually reviewing their own policies and practices to see if they meet the needs of the customer. And they look for ways to give the customer not just what it wants—but more. It may take a little more time, effort or investment in the beginning, but Turbocharged Companies have found this approach pays rich rewards, in satisfied, repeat customers.

TURBOTIP

Revering the Customer means making it easy for them to do business with you.

"What if Your Customer . . . ?"

What if your customers were in your board room when decisions about a new billing system were being discussed? What if your customers were in the sales manager's office when sales goals were being established? What if your customers could listen into the weekly meeting of the customer service staff? Does this make you feel a little uneasy?

If yours is a Turbocharged Company, the thought of your customers listening to, or even sitting in on, such a meeting would be welcome. After all, the decisions being made are in the best interest of those customers. There is no "We're going to do it this way, and they're just going to have to like it." Nor is there any "You'll just have to get more sales from ABC Company. Can't we overship a little to get their volume up?" Or, "Let's redesign the product with cheaper, less durable materials. The customer won't be able to tell the difference!"

To Turbocharged Companies, the questions are, "How can we give ABC Company the billing system they want, and also provide some extra reports they have not even thought of?" "How can we change our internal system, so that one person has all the information at his or her fingertips when a customer calls with a problem or question?" Or, "What else can we do to enhance ABC's experience in doing business with us?"

If your company would be very nervous if a customer was a "fly on the wall" and could overhear a conversation or meeting, that should be a red flag. If the subject being discussed is not in the best interest of the customer, it is not—in the long term—in the best interest of the company. If you are not sure how your customers would react, find out. Survey your customers, or go out and talk one-on-one with them. Hold a Customer Feedback Forum, where customers are invited to meet and talk with representatives of the company on a wide variety of items. Taking the pro-active approach—and acting on that information—enables you to "walk the talk." You not only say you listen to your customers, you actively go out and solicit their input.

Sure, we know it will take time, and even a small investment, to get this kind of information. Yet we challenge you—isn't it better to spend a few weeks and a few dollars up front to design and implement a new process effectively, rather than introduce something that does not meet your customers' needs? Without this, you might implement a process that is a hindrance to your customers. If this happened, you might have to scrap the entire process and start all over again.

Turbocharged Companies, however, have learned that their customer is their greatest ally. They know that a satisfied customer is the key to a successful, healthy business—and that bottom line results accompany such a relationship. Turbocharged Customers do *not* do things behind their customers' backs, instead, they actively encourage customer input and interaction wherever and whenever possible.

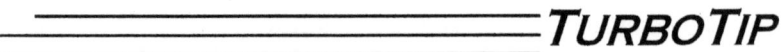

TURBOTIP

Before finalizing a business decision, ask everyone involved whether their recommendation would change if some or all of your customers were present. If the answer is yes, change your decision.

Stay in Touch

In the dynamic business world in which we find ourselves today, nothing stands still. Companies cannot merely listen to the needs of the marketplace, answer those needs and sit back. For not only will competition quickly catch up, but the customers' needs will change as well.

Take Hewlett-Packard, for example. Innovation is the name of the game with this flexible dynamo, well known for its PC printers. They barely have one product out the door before they start work on its successor. But what is truly inspirational, is the close attention they pay to the marketplace.

> *Realizing the increased trend in work from offices in the home, and hearing customers talk about the fax machine, computer printer and copy machine that have to be balanced—both on the desk and in the budget—HP came up with an answer. Their OfficeJet[i] entry into the multifunction device market puts the fax machine, the computer printer and a plain bond paper copier all in one machine. The machine is slightly larger than the desktop printer, but costs considerably less than the three machines combined.*

No doubt, HP would probably not have introduced this product had it not always been searching the marketplace for new customer needs and situations.[34]

---

[i] OfficeJet is a trademark of Hewlett-Packard Company

Home Depot has built its organization around listening, and responding to the customer. District Manager Stan Winnik states, "Once our employees have been trained and have developed an understanding of our business, they learn to keep looking for new ways to satisfy our customers, new trends. They are the cause of our constant flex and change. We are not asking them to change—they are asking us! They're coming to us with new ideas."

For your company to truly Revere Its Customers, it is essential to constantly update your knowledge about the marketplace, and customers' needs. To do this, employees must be in regular contact with customers, and must *continuously* solicit their input—so that your organization can be energized to respond to them.

TURBOTIP

You may believe you are doing everything possible to sell the customer your product. It will be much easier, however, if you *know* exactly what they want to buy.

Don't Keep Secrets

Maytag goes out of its way to tell you that the lonely old repairman is anxiously awaiting your call and the opportunity to be of service. Some hotels put notices both in the lobby and in the individual rooms assuring guests their stay will be pleasant, or they do not pay. Some automakers take extra pains to advertise voluntary recalls on their products. Why? Because they are telling the world they stand behind their promise of customer satisfaction. They are reinforcing to the customer that a wise purchasing decision was made. And they are letting potential customers know exactly the type of customer service they can expect when they purchase the company's products or utilize its services. Communicating with your customers and potential customers is important. Word will spread when you are doing a great job in customer satisfaction, but it spreads quite a bit faster when you tell people about it. It shows you have nothing to hide, and will do what you say you will.

Eastman Chemical Company has always had as its top priority meeting its customers' needs with top-quality products and services. To underscore this commitment, the company placed itself on a track to qualify for and win, in 1993, the most prestigious quality award available—the Malcolm Baldrige National Quality Award. Eastman freely admits that the scrutiny required to win such an award was grueling and intense. Yet it freely underwent this process so that it could proclaim to present and future customers, employees and others, that the company's products and processes were second to none. It was confirmation for Eastman employees who searched for ways to do things better. As Earnie Deavenport, Jr., Chairman and CEO, says, "No company achieves quality by simply concentrating on processes or equipment. It takes highly motivated people, committed to quality." In an ad announcing the award, Eastman stated, "Earning the Malcolm Baldrige National Quality Award was the hardest thing Eastman has ever done. And, for our customers, we'd do it again tomorrow."[35]

All the messages your company sends out—be they oral, written or video—should underscore your commitment to customer satisfaction. Southwest Airlines not only spends a great percentage of its annual report telling you how great their customer service is, they also show you. In their 1993 annual report, there is a center page fold-out of one of their new 737 planes. The plane is dedicated to the unsung heroes—those Southwest employees who go above and beyond the call of duty. The reader is left with the indelible impression that this company is quite serious about customer service and satisfaction.

If you are doing a great job, tell the world. Not only does it let customers and potential customers know, it makes it all that much more difficult for your competition to catch up. After all, being a "me, too" company can only earn a very distant second place.

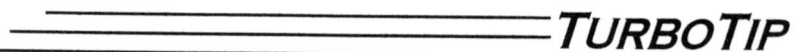

TURBOTIP

While actions clearly speak louder than words, take every opportunity to tell customers that their satisfaction is your highest priority.

Is the Customer Always Right?

While it is essential to Revere the Customer, most Turbocharged Companies do not go so far as to say the "customer is *always* right." To John Correnti at Nucor, the philosophy is simple, "The customer is always right until you discover he or she is wrong." Colleen Barrett, EVP of Customers at Southwest Airlines, agrees. "Each situation is different," she says. "The customer is always given the benefit of the doubt, but you've got to draw the line. Sometimes the customer is complaining about things totally out of our control, like the weather. In other situations, the customer does not understand the type of service we provide and is asking for more than we can deliver (meals, first-class seating, reserved seats)." Southwest's guidelines for handling customer conflicts are:

* Ask for the facts from the customer's perspective.

* Go to the employee and ask for his or her perspective on what happened.

* Attempt to give every customer a personalized, specific answer.

* Make a judgment call—Was the customer right or wrong?

* If the customer is wrong, explain why.

* Never tolerate customers abusing employees.

Progressive is in the automobile insurance business. Many of its dealings with customers occur after an accident. Progressive's approach is to be fair, and promptly pay what is owed. "You can't say the customer is always right; there are too many emotions involved. People have just suffered a financial loss and may be expecting more than is fair, reasonable and in line with their policy. We are running a business. We have a responsibility to all policy holders and stockholders, not just a single customer," states Peter Lewis, Progressive's CEO.

Finally, while every company must strive to Revere its Customers, this does not mean that companies must "give their products away." Businesses are entitled to, and require, fair remuneration for their products or services. If a business does not make a fair return, it is not upholding its responsibilities to its employees or its shareholders. Companies are not being remiss when they refuse to sell their product or service at less than a fair price, or to customers who refuse to pay their bills.

Revering the Customer means building your business around serving your customers' needs. In rare circumstances, however, a unilateral "the customer is always right" policy may not serve the needs of the customer or the company.

TURBOTIP

Unfortunately, customers who do not reciprocate the respect and integrity to which you are committed must sometimes be asked to take their business elsewhere, so that you can focus on Revering Customers who do appreciate your dedication to them.

The Lessons of Revering Your Customer

Revering Your Customer means placing customer satisfaction ahead of everything else. This is done by:

Looking At Your Customers A Little Differently—Customers are the reason for your business, not an outlet for your product. View profit as a by-product of customer satisfaction

Eliminate The "Sales" Department—Change your focus from selling to serving your customer's needs.

Assure Customer Satisfaction—Don't just aim to meet your customer's needs, strive to exceed them; don't do things behind customers' backs; and don't inconvenience customers, even if it seems beneficial for the company.

Create The Maytag Syndrome—Customers' needs should be a welcome part of every day, rather than an inconvenience.

Stay In Touch—Customers' needs are always changing, and your organization must keep adapting to those needs.

Don't Keep Secrets—Let your customers know in words, as well as deeds, that their satisfaction is your organization's number one goal.

Foundation Three—
RELENTLESSLY PURSUE PRODUCTIVITY

THE
T̲URBOCHARGED C̲OMPANY
PROCESS

UNLEASH PEOPLE POWER

REVERE CUSTOMERS

RELENTLESSLY PURSUE PRODUCTIVITY

DOMINATE MICRONICHE

OUTPERFORM COMPETITORS

SUPERIOR RETURNS ON SHAREHOLDERS' EQUITY

Unleashing People Power and Revering Customers naturally leads to Relentlessly Pursuing Productivity—the endless search for ways to perform better, faster, more effectively and at a lower cost. Unleashed employees will be motivated to find ways to enhance productivity. And the commitment to Revering Customers further focuses the organization to becoming more productive, so that customers do not have to pay for inefficiencies.

Change is the Only Constant

Turbocharged Companies know that Unleashing People Power and Revering Their Customers is not enough. Today's customers want more. They want quality products at the lowest possible price. For years, many companies simply stated, "You can't have it both ways—you either get quality or you get price." The customers, however, would not be deterred. You and I expect the highest quality at the lowest possible price when we go to retail stores to purchase a microwave, a PC, a washer or a dryer. Should our customers accept anything less?

French physiologist Claude Bernard once wrote, "Our ideas are only intellectual instruments which we use to break into phenomena; we must change them when they have served their purpose, as we change a blunt lancer that we have used long enough." Ideas are not institutions; they are not meant to stand for all times. Yet for all too many companies, yesterday's ideas or procedures become today's institutionalized way of doing business. Dying companies often sing the same chorus—"But that's the way we've always done it!" Entrenched in traditional processes, reams of manuals and familiar products, they ignore the fact that the market, indeed the entire world, is changing. Nothing stands still. In today's marketplace, doing business the way you have always done it is not a sign of a strengthened company. Instead, it is a sign of a company with its head in the sand!

In contrast, Jack Welch, Chairman and CEO of General Electric, has spent much of his time shaking things up at GE. He continues on a crusade to get managers to "Work-Out," his expression for the process of taking work out of work. He wants more efficiency and less waste. He abhors bureaucracy. Process after process has been reviewed, revised and streamlined. Work has been made simpler. The old "tried and true" ways have been replaced with efficiency, significant cost reductions and customer satisfaction. "If you can't sell a top quality product at the world's lowest price, you are going to be out of the game," Mr. Welch has stated on more than one occasion.[36] The result—his approach has brought GE from a lumbering giant to a lean global leader.[37] Thomas Edison would certainly not recognize the company he founded so many years ago.

And what Jack Welch has spearheaded at GE is what every company must do today to stay competitive. Every company's customers are continually demanding more and more of their vendors. Some companies lament, "It can't be done." Others, rethinking the process from start to finish, are changing to become more productive—endlessly searching for ways to perform better, faster, more effectively and at a lower cost. The methods being employed are almost revolutionary. We will be examining a few of these success stories to let you in on some of this radical thinking.

The obvious question might be, why? Why is Jack Welch changing GE so much? Why be so concerned about redoing things? The answer lies in the reality that, in business, you can lead—or you can follow. Leaders set the pace, followers complain about it. By being the innovator and leader, you are often in the enviable position of being the low-cost competitor. Your efficiency allows you to lower your selling price (if market forces so dictate), and still ensure yourself a fair and equitable profit on each sale. You are no longer in the position of responding to someone else's pricing decisions—you set them for everyone else.

If your organization is doing things the same way it did two years ago, there is probably a better, more productive, less costly way to do the same job. Chances are that you will not only be able to lower your costs, you will also be able to improve your quality and service to your customer as well. To look at this effectively, however, you and your colleagues are going to have to look at things very differently. Get past the rhetoric, past the security blanket of the familiar, past the comfort of the past—and be ready to blaze bold new paths.

All this may sound like a pitch for one of the newest business fads, process re-engineering. This particular fad probably has received more attention than anything since *In Search of Excellence,*[i] back in 1982. Like most miracle cures, however, process re-engineering has left many an unsatisfied user and critic in its wake. Magazine articles on fixing the process abound, and "how-to" books illustrating techniques for repairing the re-engineering process overflow from virtually all business book sections.

We believe, however, process re-engineering does have an important place in a business that is receptive to, and ready for, change. No, not as a cure-all for every single business problem. But, executed within the context of Unleashing Employees, Revering Customers and Relentlessly Pursuing Productivity in order to Dominate your MicroNiche, it can be extremely valuable. Not as a stand-alone program, but as part of a total company treatment. Not something that requires a huge manual to implement or armies of consultants, but a way of life that becomes the daily culture of the organization. If your organization is like GE was, entrenched in decades of red tape and bureaucracy, then a more serious and structured approach to reviewing every job and process is in order. If, however, your organization is more like Southwest Airlines or Nucor, where rethinking processes and procedures have always been part of the culture, then this process is different. In this latter circumstance, the process becomes more spotting an opportunity to improve productivity and forming a "posse" to attack the problem, then regrouping and doing it all over again.

---

[i] Copyright © 1982 by Thomas J. Peters and Robert H. Waterman, Jr.

During the time immediately preceding the publication of this book, we worked with nearly a dozen companies who pursued process re-engineering extensively. Each one saw benefit from the program. Yet each company also realized that it was more than this one program alone that would be required to completely transform their business into a successful enterprise.

Process re-engineering sounds like technical, formal, white lab coat type material. We prefer to look at it for what it is—a tool to ensure the organization Relentlessly Pursues Productivity to attain or maintain its lowest cost, most productive position.

Relentlessly Pursuing Productivity allows you to truly Revere your Customer. It enables your company to provide the maximum value for each dollar your customer spends. Embracing change and continually challenging the status quo are essential parts of the culture of Turbocharged Companies.

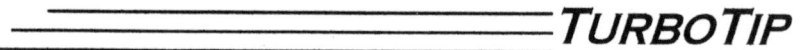

TURBOTIP

"We've always done it this way" is the best justification for critically reviewing a process or procedure.

Do It Every Two Years

Most processes and procedures in force in business today have been cobbled together over several years, by a number of people. All these creators were well-intentioned—they only wanted to make the process better. Not wanting, or having enough time, to change the entire procedure, these do-gooders merely amended this, amplified that, and modified something else. Each time the process got more complicated, as it is rare that elements are ever discarded—instead, things generally are added to the process or procedure. The end result, more often than not, is a tremendous amount of inefficiency.

Our rule of thumb is "Do It Every Two Years." All major processes and procedures should be reviewed at least every two years. In today's environment, technology changes so fast, it is impossible to stand still. Today's next generation computer will be tomorrow's old "has-been" system. Materials change, specifications change, ideas change. You need to be on the forefront of those changes to remain the low-cost producer.

If the concept of reviewing things every two years sounds ludicrous, think about this. Freudenberg-NOK is a supplier of O-Rings to Chrysler Corporation. Since 1992, it has embraced a faster, leaner, cheaper mentality. It has been holding productivity improvement/cost reduction workshops throughout the company, often with Chrysler executives in attendance. In 1993 alone, this supplier cut production lead-time in half, increased productivity 52 percent, reduced work-in-progress inventory by 85 percent and reduced required floor space by 30 percent, while slicing cycle time by 78 percent. Scrap even shrunk by 17 percent.[38] Savings amounted to $6 to $8 million in direct costs for that year alone! The place had to be running at peak efficiency—nothing more to be done—right?

Well, the following year, 31 more teams combed through the plant. Vice President of Chrysler Technology and Rental Car Operations Joseph Cappy was on a team that examined vacuum pumps that are used on the O-Ring molding presses. They noted that four molding presses ran off one vacuum pump, while a second pump was used as a back-up. But by utilizing both pumps, the team found they could reduce downtime by 50 percent and reduce defects by about 30 percent; this, in a plant that had seen phenomenal strides in productivity during the past two years. Scores of teams had ferreted out every ounce of inefficiency—or so they thought. Yet the savings continue to mount as each team goes through the plant.[39] Noting the success its supplier has experienced with productivity enhancements and cost savings, Robert Eaton, Chrysler's Chairman and CEO declared, "We will not rest knowing that we're already the industry's lowest cost producer, because we believe there is still a lot of waste that can come out." Chrysler continues to study, and restudy, every area for productivity enhancements and cost improvements.[40]

Having decided that your organization needs to examine itself to realize the benefits of improved efficiency, where do you begin? We suggest that the first step is to identify a process to review. Perhaps it is quoting, order processing, raw material procurement, receiving, accounts payable, accounts receivable or collections. It is important that whatever this process is, it be something you can "get your arms around." Achieving a 20 percent return for the shareholders is a lofty goal, but not a process that can be evaluated, for example.

Once the process to be evaluated has been defined, a self-managed work team should be established to tackle the problem. We have found that, where practical, having representatives from all the impacted areas is quite important. In this manner, the team is not operating in an information vacuum. Further, we encourage that no more than 40 percent of the team come from management ranks. This ensures the results will not be predisposed toward management's viewpoint. Additional guidelines in establishing teams can be found in the section of this book relating to the First Foundation—Unleashing People Power, and in Appendix "A."

The team leader should then be appointed by management or elected by the team. This person facilitates the meetings, obtains the necessary information and spearheads the implementation of the team's recommendations. Remember, this person is not the "boss" of the team—he or she does not even have to be a manager. What is important is this person's ability to work with a variety of people—to spark creativity and gain consensus—while having the tenacity to see recommendations through.

The team then meets to tackle the problem. This is a two-part process. To begin, the existing process must be documented and measured. It is important to note not only what happens in a general sense, but each and every step, each "thing" that happens along the way. The process must be examined from the level of detail a new person would require if assigned to do that task, having never done it before. Items to review include, but are not limited to:

The number of hand-offs—The number of times materials, information or documents are given to another person.

The number of duplicate steps—Where one employee basically duplicates the work of another. For example, if a sales person writes an order on an order form, which is then entered by someone else into a computer, duplication takes place. The same information is being communicated—handled—more than one time.

The distance traveled—In a manufacturing environment, this is the distance materials travel from the receiving dock through all the various processes, until it is loaded onto an outbound truck for shipment.

The number of pieces of paper produced—And the time it takes to complete the paperwork.

The number of pieces of paper retained by the company—And what is done with them.

The elapsed time from the beginning to the end of the process.

The amount of value-added, non-value-added and waiting time—For our purposes, we will define value-added time as that time when someone is doing something of measurable value to the customer. Time, for example, that an engineer spends designing something to fit a particular customer's set of needs. Non-value-added time is that time during which the customer receives nothing of measurable value. An example would be the time spent looking for inventory to fill an order. Finally, waiting time is time when nothing happens. Examples include the order that is sitting on the credit manager's desk, waiting for approval. Or, some parts are sitting on the assembly line, but cannot be put together because other necessary parts have not yet arrived.

Once this information and documentation has been gathered, the process can then be analyzed and recommendations for improvement made. The team must review each step, constantly asking itself if this step is really necessary, and if so, how it can be done better, faster and at a lower cost. When Chrysler examines a process, it sets goals for improvement, but it also sets a stretch goal for improving that process by at least 50 percent. While it does not always make that lofty goal, the company always makes progress, improves the process—and learns. This allowed, for example, the company to reduce the time needed to make and deliver a car from 68 days to 37. Teams need to review how processes can be made simpler. How hand-offs can be reduced. How unnecessary steps, duplication of effort, or paperwork can be eliminated.

As we related earlier, Chrysler's efforts in reviewing processes brought about a significant change in its product development area. Traditionally, automakers have set teams of engineers, designers, production planners, suppliers and others working on a new model car in complete isolation from one another—often competing with one another. Chrysler now puts all these disparate groups together in a Platform Team. Instead of problems being worked out on the assembly line, they are now worked out at the water cooler or in hallway conversations. Instead of being spread across various buildings and floors, they sit a few feet from one another. This process enabled Chrysler to bring out its Ram pickup in 32 months and its Neon automobile in 31 months. Compare that with the nearly 60 months it takes most of the other automakers. Not only are the costs significantly less and the product far superior, it enables Chrysler to be less of a fortune teller, trying to decide what consumers will want five years from now.

One of our clients, a manufacturer of steel products, reviewed its manufacturing process. It discovered that its materials traveled 1500 yards from the receiving dock to the shipping dock, were subjected to 14 hand-offs and were in the plant for 90 days. By carefully modifying the process, it was able to reduce the travel to 150 yards, five hand-offs and seven days of elapsed time—resulting in a 15 percent reduction in overall product cost, and substantially improved customer response time.

If the team was originally charged with the authorization to implement their ideas, they are then free to begin this process as soon they are ready. If, however, their mandate requires management approval[i] before implementation, then their ideas and recommendations would be presented to management, who should be prepared to respond on the spot. No "Very interesting, we'll take the idea and study it to death." No large report, bound in leather, that serves more as a doorstop than a collection of ideas. Instead, just a simple presentation detailing the process, the pitfalls, the recommendations and the implementation costs and schedule. Once approved, it is the team leader's job to ensure the recommendations are implemented as described. To do this may require reassembling the team from time to time to review

---

[i] For additional discussion on this subject, see Foundation One, Establishing Work Teams chapter.

145

recommendations in light of new information, or to assist in the implementation process. Then the process starts all over again.

It is also important to note that teams need to communicate with one another, and with the organization at large. Chrysler's Bob Eaton puts it this way: "Good ideas that aren't shared are wasted ideas, and wasted ideas are no better than bad ideas. A team that produces a successful vehicle, but doesn't share what it learned, and the mistakes it made, with the other teams, is a failure."[41] In much the same manner, "springing" a radical change on an organization does not help gain acceptance by the people who must work with the change each and every day. Communication is vital to change.

Not all changes require radical surgery. SIFCO Forge Group decided to examine their price quoting process. What they found was this:

> *When a job came in for quotation, the company went to great lengths to ensure the quotation was as accurate as possible. The estimating department sent inquiries to various departments about how long this or that would take. Purchasing received a daily deluge of three-part requests for quotation for every item the company would need to purchase from outside vendors. Being efficient purchasing types, three requests for quotation were generated and faxed out to various suppliers.*

> *When the quotes were received, they were reviewed and forwarded to estimating with the appropriate notations. The estimating department would then compile all the necessary data and generate a quotation. Total elapsed time—16 days. Total value-added time— three hours; the rest was waiting time.*

> *The team assigned to this task reviewed all the necessary information, documenting the process and enumerating the detailed efforts. After some intensive brainstorming (and a little research), the team made two significant discoveries. First, the company only won about 15 percent of its quotes. Second, the vast majority*

of the quotes won involved significant negotiations after the job had been quoted. It turned out that the customers were not looking for, nor expecting a formal, cast-in-concrete quotation. They were still making changes. They did want, however, a fairly accurate "ballpark" price on what this job would cost.

Armed with this information, the team completely revamped the process. Suppliers were asked to provide a standard price list, that would be used for "ballpark" quotations only. When contracts were won, and details more sure, more formal quotations would then be sought. The overall estimating process was reduced from 16 days to just three. Internal paperwork was reduced by 90 percent. Two positions in purchasing were eliminated, and additional clerical time was saved. The end result was not only a great cost savings to the company, but a significant competitive advantage. While all its competitors were busy faxing out requests for quotation and analyzing them, our client was transmitting its quote to the customer.

Remember, if you have a process in your company that has been in place for two years or more, it is time to have a look at it. You can undoubtedly make some changes, smooth out some work flows or eliminate unnecessary procedures, resulting in greater productivity. This will help move your organization toward becoming the low-cost provider.

TURBOTIP

Every process in your business can be improved. Don't miss the chance to discover these opportunities.

Doing It Right the First Time

There is an old saying that goes, "You never seem to have the time to do it right the first time, but you always have the time to do it over again." This business practice feeds on itself. If you are rushing to get a project done to make a deadline, only to have to spend additional time reworking the project to make it right, you have all that much less time on the next project. Chances are the next project will need some degree of rework as well, so the cycle just continues. And each time, companies incur the increased costs to correct an error that should never have occurred in the first place.

Human beings are happy when they feel a sense of accomplishment in what they are doing. Employees do not feel they have done their best when they are rushed to get the job out the door, for the sense of pride in what they are doing goes out the door as well. The sense of "ownership" in the product, process or service disappears; in fact, the employees often do not want to be associated with the work done. It is the exact opposite of everything we have talked about thus far. Lack of employee ownership, lack of pride, and frustration all translate into higher scrap rates, higher product rejection rates, and higher levels of customer complaints. And all this heaps additional cost onto the product or service, destroying any competitive advantage the company might have otherwise enjoyed.

Worse than rushing to get a job done is trying to do your best, but not really knowing whether or not you are doing the job correctly. At SIFCO, the metal forge shop was experiencing higher and higher levels of rejected parts. These errors were detected, as is typical with most companies, at the *end* of the operation. At that point, the work of not only the forge operators, but the machinists, grinders and polishers was all for naught. Understandably, everyone involved in the process was becoming more and more frustrated.

Most traditional companies would have added more quality control inspectors. They would have inspected the product at both the beginning and the end of the process. That is the typical response—and it does have some merit. At SIFCO, this idea was considered, but rejected. This idea would not only have generated additional expense, it would have necessitated 100 percent inspection of every part immediately after the forging operation. The expense and time required for doing this was enormous.

The company's process re-engineering team took up the challenge and determined there was a much easier and more cost-effective way to solve this problem. Instead of adding a fleet of inspectors, they designed a relatively simple template for the forge hammer operators. In this manner, the accuracy of each part coming off the press could be immediately checked at the *beginning* of the process. This change would significantly reduce the chance for any part's rejection when it underwent final inspection. The machinist's time, the grinder's time and the buffer's time were now dedicated to parts that should pass inspection.

With this improvement in the process, the hammer operators felt better about what they were doing—they were no longer in the dark. They knew they were passing good parts to the next team and were proud of it. The machining, grinding and buffing teams felt better about their work because they knew the parts they received were good, and that they were adding value to that part. They were not wasting their time, which they felt they had been doing previously. Finally, costs per part were significantly reduced as the reject rate plummeted and the amount of quality product produced per shift skyrocketed. This in turn lead to increased on-time deliveries, which certainly pleased SIFCO's customers. Note that no additional work was being done here to accelerate production in order to meet customer delivery schedules. Because the process was examined, and modifications made, all the work being produced had a significantly better chance of making it through the process than it did under the old method.

When trying to improve their product quality, most traditional thinking companies instinctively respond with "We'll beef-up Quality Control." While we are certainly not about to tell you to abolish Quality Control departments, we will tell you that this reflex action is not always the panacea it would seem. Simply installing or increasing Quality Control departments can never address pride in workmanship. If non-Unleashed, non-Customer Revering employees know they have to "get it by" the inspector, they will often do only the bare minimum necessary to meet that standard. Or, they may let work go through their work station that really should not, reasoning that "they'll catch it down the line." As a result, scrap and rework costs escalate. Increasing the QC staff might actually be working against you.

In a Turbocharged Company, Unleashed, motivated employees want to produce good, quality products. They have pride in signing off on the work they have done. They are not worried about getting work past the final inspection; because they know that final inspector doesn't work for the company—he or she is the customer. They want the customer to be satisfied—even delighted—with the products they produce, or the services they render. It is this type of attitude that means so much more to a company's efficiency and quality than any forced quality control program could ever do. Quality control does have its place—as an independent verification of work performed at or above standard. It never should be viewed as a police officer, or a quality *fix*, because the *fixing* is in the hands of the employees making the product or providing the service. SIFCO's Mark Wanderslaben, an hourly employee who was a vital member of the team responsible for the turnaround plan, states, "When you Unleash People Power, people police themselves. There is enormous pride in what is going on. People don't let slackers get by."

Sometimes, doing it right the first time means looking at the function to determine if there is an easier way to do the job. Instead of relying on an order picker to remember which version of which part goes to which customer in which state, why not rely on the computer? It can be programmed to calculate all these boring variables much faster and more accurately than relying on human memories.

The appropriate design of Gainsharing Plans can be of significant help in this area. If the plan rewards employees for productivity, they will be motivated to search for ways to organize their processes in order to achieve quality products the first time, because they will quickly discover that the cost of reworking parts or other production inefficiencies is costing *them* money.

Doing It Right the First Time means examining processes to determine a way to ensure a better product or service from the effort expended. It means giving people the time and resources they need to do the job right, thereby significantly decreasing the amount of time they spend on rework or quality problems. Doing It Right the First Time makes everyone's efforts more productive, and lets people feel proud of what they do.

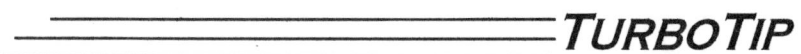

TURBOTIP

While *practice makes perfect* in many arenas, business processes must be *done right the first time* in order to maximize productivity.

Work Smarter, Not Harder

Today's Turbocharged Companies have learned to work much *smarter*, rather than much harder. They have learned to do the right things, not to do things right. They have challenged the "but that's the way we've always done it" mentality and come up with a better solution. In a Turbocharged Company environment, being "leaner" means working "smarter."

At Chrysler, keeping costs down is an important priority. When you are making 600,000 minivans each year, for instance, saving even one dollar per vehicle can make a significant bottom line contribution. And that is only one of Chrysler's product lines.

Chrysler realized that 70 percent of what goes into each vehicle they sell is manufactured by someone else—their suppliers. From this knowledge began the Supplier Cost Reduction Effort, or SCORE program. Under this program, Chrysler listens to suggestions and ideas that come from its suppliers—a program that has generated over 9,700 ideas in the last three years, resulting in more than $1.1 billion in savings.[42] Many of its suppliers are full-time members of the Platform Teams that design each new or revised car and truck. Detroit, listening to its suppliers' ideas—even encouraging them? Outrageous, you cry? Well, it does not stop there.

After establishing an atmosphere that encouraged free and open communications, Chrysler took the next important step. It abolished the old competitive bid purchasing system and replaced it with a target costing plan.

Under target costing, the final price for a car or truck is established by determining what the consumer would be willing to pay for the finished vehicle. From this, the process works in reverse to determine the price for each part. Vendors are told which components or systems are required; their functions, performance levels and quality levels; and the price Chrysler is willing to pay for this part, which is ultimately what the consumer is willing to pay for the part. The vendor then has free rein to design the component within these specifications.

The results have been all that could be hoped for and more. Each of Chrysler's last four product introductions came in at hundreds of dollars below target costs. That translates to more value for the customer for less money.[43]

Imagine that—a system where everyone works a little smarter, rethinking the traditional way of doing things. It allows Chrysler and its suppliers to work together, not against one another. Each can make a reasonable profit, and each has a good feeling about what it is doing. How many companies can say that, as more and more pressure is exerted on containing costs?

At Progressive Insurance, emphasis is placed on quick response to customers who have been involved in accidents. They underscore their core value of providing fast, fair, empathetic and personal response to claims reports with a variety of services. These services start with a 24 hour-a-day national claims service toll-free number where accidents can be reported, and from which claims assistance can be dispatched. On any given evening scores of adjusters are on call across the country in order to provide the service consumers want but often do not receive from their insurance companies. Each adjuster's company vehicle is equipped with a laptop computer and cellular telephone—in short, everything the adjuster needs to do his/her job. The adjuster can even write a check at the scene of an accident.

Chuck Chokel, CFO of Progressive, reports that "Faster response actually results in savings because people appreciate your service and know you care. They don't feel it is their right to steal from you. From our standpoint, the facts about the accident are easier to establish, memories are fresher and important evidence has not had a chance to become lost."

Progressive's innovative ideas have certainly caught the eyes of consumers, as Progressive enjoyed a 35 percent increase in policy premiums written during 1994, when compared with the previous year. Progressive's practices even saved the company money, while allowing it to be more responsive and sensitive to customers' needs.

Finally, Nucor's lean management structure is almost legendary in the steel industry. This $3 billion steel producer has just four levels of management and 5,700 employees. As we mentioned earlier, its home office has less than 25 people—and the "company dining room" is the luncheonette across the street

James Coblin, Nucor's Manager of Personnel Services, tells of the instructions given to new managers when they ask what they are supposed to do. First, they are told, do not manage anything. Don't write letters or call meetings. Do, however, go into the plant and observe what is going on. Don't say anything, or mess anything up, and if you do this properly, someone will eventually ask you a question. This is your time to shine. Answer the question to the very best of your ability—put your heart and soul into the answer. For "when employees ask [you] questions, it means they are ready to receive [your] input." This is the function of management.[44]

It is obvious that with management spread so thin, Nucor could not expect managers to perform traditional managerial duties. Instead, by empowering its employees, it uses managers as coaches and counselors. As Kevin Young, the Cold Mill Manager at the company's Crawfordsville, Indiana operation, puts it, "It is a lot easier to lead than it is to manage. You don't have to baby-sit your workers. As a result, you need a lot less managers." This extremely smart approach allows Nucor to retain the enviable title as lowest cost producer in the steel industry.

While Turbocharged Companies never stop looking for ways to improve productivity and lower costs, they realize the importance of using their low-cost structure as much for offensive as defensive purposes. Sure, lower costs help fight off an aggressive competitor. The real benefit of low-cost, however, comes when a company is able to use its cost structure to facilitate growth—by entering new markets, for example. Few companies will be able to remain Turbocharged Companies for the long term if they do not grow aggressively—and only efficient players will be able to do this effectively. Growth also provides opportunities for talented individuals who, due to productivity gains, have become redundant in other areas of the organization.

Much of the time, companies harm themselves by not looking past the obvious. Turbocharged Companies, as you have seen, go well past the traditional, exploring ways to make new ideas work instead of citing reasons why they will not. They are constantly trying to make it easier and less cumbersome to get each job done. All their actions are focused on providing more value to the customer. They do not do things just because "the system" forces them.

TURBOTIP

While hard work is always admirable, businesses must continually search for ways to achieve more using substantially less "sweat." Working smarter means looking past the obvious for the better way to accomplish tasks.

Research By Any Other Name . . .

"When you steal from one author, it's plagiarism; if you steal from many, it's research."

— *Wilson Mizner*

One of the best and easiest ways to improve the efficiency within your own organization is by looking around at what other successful companies are doing. This approach, in which many consulting companies specialize, is usually referred to as "Benchmarking" or "Best Practices." A major part of the work Jack Welch has championed at General Electric involves combating the "not invented here" syndrome. GE's people were so used to being the inventors, the innovators, that they rarely looked around to see what other companies were doing. Under Welch, GE staffers began visiting other companies—in businesses similar and dissimilar to their own—to study their ideas and methods. These were then incorporated at GE wherever possible.

In GE's 1991 annual report, Welch recognized the lessons learned from those companies—particularly Wal-Mart. "Many of our management teams spend time there observing the speed, the bias for action, the utter customer fixation that drives Wal-Mart; and despite our progress, we came back feeling a bit plodding and ponderous, a little envious, but ultimately, fiercely

157

determined that we're going to do whatever it takes to get there fast."

GE has made a lot of progress since then. Best Practices facilitated the development of Quick Response—GE's just-in-time inventory management system. Now other companies are visiting GE, to see how they can learn from GE's success.[45]

Chrysler's Robert Eaton echoes these sentiments when he states, " . . .we have people on airplanes almost every day, traveling to other companies to study the way those companies manage their processes. We're looking at the Best Practices of the best companies all over the world, and if it makes sense for us, we're adopting them. The old 'not invented here' syndrome is not appreciated at Chrysler . . .We're not too proud to ask for help when we see somebody doing something better than we do it, and we're generous enough to share what we've learned with those who ask us for help."[46]

Boeing's 777 was produced in a radically different way than the airline industry had ever experienced. Not only were suppliers involved in the initial design stages, but potential customers and even frequent flyers as well. Allied Signal, a supplier of a wide array of products for this new aircraft, including the auxiliary power unit (APU), reported that over 100 airline industry suggestions[47] were incorporated into the final design of the APU alone. This exchange of views and ideas certainly heralded a new era in the aerospace industry.

For years, U.S. companies bitterly complained because foreign competition came in, looked at our products and examined how they were made. They then took the best ideas back with them, tossed out everything else and significantly cut the cost of the manufactured product. If we are to learn anything from this experience, it is that pride comes from providing what the customer wants—and more—at a profit rate that allows the company to prosper and provides shareholders with a reasonable return on their investment. Pride does not come from re-inventing something that already exists just to be able to say it is "yours."

Pride is giving your customer the product he wants, at the lowest possible price. In this manner everyone wins.

The lessons here are clear. First, get rid of the "not invented here" syndrome. Swallow your pride. If someone else has a good idea, or a better way to do something, copy it. Don't reinvent the wheel each time. Second, and just as important, break new ground, not ground already broken. Encourage your team to devote its time and energy to getting further ahead, not reinventing. Steer your employees to focusing their efforts on areas others have not perfected. By doing these two things, your company will not only be better off, but your employees will feel their talents are being utilized to the maximum benefit of the company, its customers, and themselves.

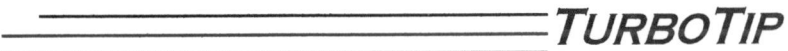 *TURBOTIP*

There is no need to re-invent the wheel. If someone else has already figured out a better way to execute a given task, there is no shame in learning from that experience.

Take the Paperless Challenge

W hen we hear someone boast about the "good deal" he or she received on the purchase of additional file cabinets, we shudder. Business today seems to love paper—we cannot seem to get enough of it. To be sure, we automate processes, build data bases and spend untold billions on computers, ostensibly to eliminate paper. Yet each year, more and more file cabinets become filled with more tons of paper. One copy machine company, in touting their new copier, published an ad with a headline stating it is capable of producing some incredible number of copies each year. The next line in the ad, tongue in cheek, states, "Great, more paperwork." While, on one hand, Americans abhor cutting down trees needlessly, we will go out and make 25 more copies with the other.

This reliance on paper, on files, on even printing computer screens is not only maddening, it is terribly inefficient. It wastes time, materials, energy and floor space. A recent study by a research firm found that the average office worker makes 21 trips per day to the fax machine, the printer, the copier and the file cabinets. The total daily trips are the equivalent of one hour of wandering around per employee! That means 12-1/2 percent of each employee's day is wasted chasing paper. Strictly by the numbers, by eliminating all this paper chasing, you could eliminate one out of every eight employees you have[48]—or free them to work on more productive activities. Suddenly a few sheets of copy paper take on a very significant cost factor.

Turbocharged Companies realize the importance of substantially reducing the production and retention of paper. Paper is often just a crutch used by employees intimidated by the computer, where most of the information resides anyway. Even worse, having two data bases—one paper and one electronic—virtually guarantees that neither will be totally inclusive or correct. Each employee dictates, by his or her preference, which data base will be the most up-to-date.

A team at Progressive Corporation realized that this "security with paper" crutch existed, and that some degree of retraining would be necessary to eliminate reliance on paper. A team was charged with reducing the number of times a customer service representative pulled a paper file. They started out by limiting access to the file cabinets to twice each day. They coupled this action with retraining employees in the ease and use of the computer system

After the training was complete, a bright yellow police line tape was placed around the file cabinets. During this phase, only phone requests for files were accepted. As the last step, the file cabinets were moved to the basement (a considerable distance away from the users), where the files were eventually destroyed.

The actions of this wise team enabled employees to rely on their electronic system, which they then began to appreciate and use more fully than ever before. Now employees had all the correct information they needed—right at their fingertips. In addition to recovering valuable office space previously tied up with filing cabinets, the team reduced the amount of time employees spent hunting for records and comparing electronic entries with paper. Not only were costs decreased, but customer service was enhanced, as inquiries could be handled "live" rather than requiring a call-back once the paper file was located.

A client of ours took a slightly different approach. The business was paper-intensive; multipart documents were created any time an inquiry was received, a delivery made, equipment returned and when invoicing or crediting a customer. All of these multi-part forms, along with various photocopies made along the way, were all stored in an ever increasing line of file cabinets.

> *Overwhelmed by paper, inefficiency and duplication of efforts, the company committed itself to the "paperless challenge." With a devotion to duty that would make even a revival meeting preacher proud, this organization achieved their goal in 90 days. In place of the rows of file cabinets, the computer system was modified to include the information previously only contained on all the various handwritten forms. Access to data was expanded to more employees, and the system made more user-friendly. Information was entered into the system once, then used by as many departments as necessary. Finally, a scanner was purchased and installed to permanently record the customers' signatures on delivery slips and credit applications. Signatures could thus be captured and stored along with the balance of the electronic data. The paper records were no longer needed, and thus could be sent off to the paper recycler. Oh yes, the file cabinets—they were sold to a less enlightened organization!*

Before we close on the paperless challenge, a few final thoughts are in order. First, automation is not a panacea—it will not cure your business ills. It will not make sloppy, inefficient practices great. It may allow you to make mistakes faster, though we are sure you will agree that is certainly not something to be desired.

It is for this reason that Southwest Airlines has always gone relatively slowly in automating a process. John Dennison, Executive Vice President for Southwest's Corporate Services, explains it this way, "Herb (Kelleher-President, Chairman & CEO) focuses more on the interpersonal part of a procedure, rather than the automation aspect. We believe that unless you really understand a procedure and how to efficiently utilize electronic assistance in that procedure, you're never going to see the benefits. The business people must drive what the computer can do for them, not the computer people."

And, while we advocate automating as many processes as possible, we acknowledge that becoming totally paperless is probably not a realistic or cost-effective goal. There will undoubtedly be, at least for the foreseeable future, the need for some paper records in any organization.

Notwithstanding any of the acknowledged limitations, we remain convinced of the merits of a substantially paperless environment. In pursuing this goal, the organization is forced to re-examine and question activities that were previously taken for granted. "Why do we generate this document?" or "Why are we making six photocopies of this invoice?" are the type of questions that surface during this process. And, when processes do become paperless, productivity and communications are greatly enhanced.

While going totally paperless may not be practical, companies should commit to reducing the reliance on paper as much as possible, in order to streamline processes, regain employee time and enhance customer service.

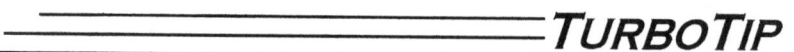 *TURBOTIP*

Businesses that do not commit themselves to become substantially "paperless" by the year 2000 will have a tough time competing in the 21st century.

Outsourcing is Not a Dirty Word

It once was the wisdom throughout corporate America that the more you could do inside, the better off you were. You could do it better, cheaper and more efficiently in-house. And in some cases, this statement is true even today. Yet we notice that an increasing number of companies are looking at their organizations and asking themselves "How did we ever get into...?"

Doing things internally often hides a lot of the costs associated with this process or product. A product which "costs" a corporation $1.00 often winds up costing much more than that when these hidden costs are factored back in. Items such as scrap, rework time, and work-in-process inventories all add up to bring that $1.00 product up to $1.35 or more. Yet outsourced, that product may only cost $1.25. "Savings" quickly evaporate when you look at the situation in this light.

Turbocharged Companies have learned to stick with their core competencies—those things they are very good at doing. And they are looking at outside vendors to handle the rest. A perfect example of this is in the data processing field. Companies are finding that it makes a lot of sense to *outboard* their data processing function to an outside concern, rather than become deeply involved in something in which they are not experts. They are not saddled with questions like "Is the equipment current?" or "Should I invest in something else?" or "Can we afford to upgrade?" Instead, they focus on running their business, and let professionals handle the rest.

One of our clients, a manufacturer of steel parts, completely outsourced its raw material procurement and management to a steel service center. Our client now carries no more inventory than can be used for production the following day. In addition to the increased Return on Assets it enjoys from this practice, our client reports lower tax levels, less congestion at the plant and increased production speed, as employees no longer have to hunt to find the materials they need.

Finally, the same outsourcing argument is making a lot of sense to companies both big and small when looking at their payroll and benefits functions. While basic payroll functions may not have changed all that much, various and changing state regulations, federal mandates and constantly changing forms have made this an area in which organizations can spend a lot of time and resources in order to stay current. In this regulatory arena, where mistakes can be very costly from a variety of standpoints, most companies are utilizing outside service companies to handle this function. The downside risk far outweighs any perceived "additional" cost.

If your company needs help in areas beyond your core competence, why not go to a firm that specializes just in that? After all, people come to your firm because of your specialized knowledge, don't they? Why invest in high-caliber professionals if that is not your core business? The "not invented here" syndrome must extend to looking at the ancillary functions your company performs and determining if there is a better way to handle these operations.

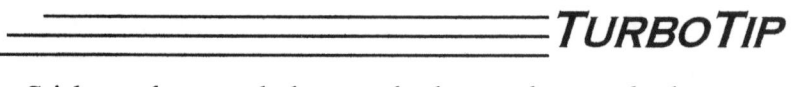

Stick to what you do best, and rely on others to do the rest.

"Oh Give Me a ROAM . . ."

When German born architect Mies van der Rohe coined the phrase "Less is more," he was referring to simple elegance in buildings. Yet the same thing can be said in business. If you can do more with less, you actually get more. Let us explain.

If two similar businesses each generate $10 million in sales each year, and Company A makes $500,000 in profit[i] while Company B makes $1 million, then Company B would seem to be the better company, right? But, if we told you that company A employed assets[ii] of $2 million to earn its $500,000 in profit, while Company B employed $8 million in assets to earn its $1 million, we might get you to change your mind. That's because of an extremely important, but little understood, principle called Return on Assets Managed or "ROAM."[iii]

In our example, Company A utilized $2 million to generate $500,000 in profit. That is a 25 percent ROAM ($500,000

---

[i] For purposes of this calculation, we define Profit as Earnings before Depreciation, Interest and Taxes.

[ii] Assets or Assets Managed is defined as the average total Assets for the period, after adding back Accumulated Depreciation. To the extent that the market value of assets differ significantly from their original cost, market value should be used instead. Some analysts deduct Accounts Payable balances from Total Assets to arrive at Assets Managed.

[iii] For a detailed discussion on ROAM, and improvement thereof, see *Corporate Intensive Care: Why Businesses Fail and How To Make Them Succeed* by Larry Goddard (York Publishing, 1993) Part One, Section III.

divided by $2 million). Company B achieved only a 14.3 percent ROAM, generating $1 million from $8 million in assets ($1 million divided by $8 million). So, bottom line, where would you want to invest your money—in a business that gave you a 25 percent return each year on your investment, or in one that provided you with only 14.3 percent? To be sure, both investments would provide more return than placing your money in a savings account, or even in a CD. But why invest in Company B when you could go out and invest in a handful of companies similar to Company A? While you consider your answer to this question for our hypothetical companies, shouldn't you also be asking this question of your own business?

Earlier, we described how Return on Shareholders' Equity (ROE) is the critical benchmark of a company's financial success. In order for management to be able to improve their ROE, they must start by focusing on improving their ROAM. Businesses can improve their ROAM by improving their operating profits— through increased sales or reduced costs—or by reducing the assets used in their operations.

Managers are provided with capital to operate the business from three major sources: 1.) shareholders' equity, 2.) interest bearing funds (*e.g.* loans, bonds, debentures), and 3.) non-interest bearing funds (*e.g.* Accounts Payable). Managers invest capital in assets (*e.g.* Inventory, Accounts Receivable, Machinery), with which they operate the business. The objective, of course, is to generate a profit (or return) from the assets they are managing. The higher the return they generate on assets they are managing, the greater the return to shareholders (ROE).

While improving ROAM via operating enhancement or asset reduction is the best, and most profitable way to increase ROE, managers can also increase ROE by changing the mix of funds from the three sources of funds mentioned above. ROE may actually be improved, provided ROAM exceeds the cost of interest bearing debt, by utilizing a higher proportion of capital from interest bearing and non-interest bearing sources—relying less on shareholders' equity, which reduces the denominator in the ROE calculation.

To be sure, some businesses are much more capital intensive than others. Yet almost every business can increase its ROAM by taking a look at one very often overlooked item—working capital. Working capital is defined as inventories—raw materials, work-in-process and finished goods—plus the company's Accounts Receivable, less its Accounts Payable. *Fortune* 500 companies, on average, require 20 cents of working capital for each dollar of sales. Yet we can tell you that many smart companies are trying to eliminate their working capital! Jack Welch, GE's determined CEO, has made working-capital reduction a crusade. He realizes that in so doing, he will not only free up cash, but also speed up production.

Reducing working capital is important for several reasons. First, every dollar released from inventories generates a one-time contribution to cash flow—cash flow that could provide the funds necessary to enhance a company's productivity (*e.g.* new, more productive machinery). Second, it permanently increases earnings, as working capital, like all capital, costs money. Cutting working inventories forces companies to produce faster, on more flexible schedules. Warehouses, once filled with inventories, can now be fitted with additional manufacturing cells, ready to respond to more customer demand. It enables you to not only be the low-cost producer, but allows you to service your customer in ways previously thought unattainable.

Traditionally, companies produce extensive long-term forecasts from which they manufacture products weeks if not months in advance. It is from these stockpiles that many manufacturers fill their customers' orders. GE's appliance business in Lexington, Kentucky was no exception to this rule, as products planned in the dead of winter would finally arrive at customer's doors in early summer.

Today, GE is tying its production to its orders, with of its manufacturing facilities making every model, every day, in incredibly small lots. This allows them to plan, produce and deliver product in one-sixth the time it previously took. As a result, inventories have been sliced in half, saving some $400 million. GE's ultimate goal in the appliance division is to make and deliver in 10 days, and further halve its inventories to $200 million.[50] That serves the customer better and the company better, and it increases the Return On Assets Managed.

Skeptics who believe reducing working capital will only work in certain industries need only look to Kelsey-Hayes of Livonia, Michigan, a subsidiary of Varity Corp. This company produces the antilock braking systems and brake components widely used on today's automobiles. From 1990 to 1993, while sales nearly doubled, manufacturing time was slashed from 30 days to just seven, and working capital has been cut from $70 million in 1990 to a negative $18 million in 1993! Today, Kelsey-Hayes begins manufacturing product only once an order is received—yet is still able to deliver products when the customers want them.[51]

Compaq Computer is also rethinking its manufacturing process by designing a flexible build-to-order manufacturing system. To do this, Compaq is utilizing the cell manufacturing process we mentioned earlier. Compaq figures this will not only enhance their operational efficiency, it will also sharply decrease its reliance on pre-built inventory like the staggering $2 billion stockpile of goods the company had amassed at the end of 1994.[52]

Alongside the reduction in working capital, companies should also implement a thorough review of the effectiveness and efficiency of machinery, equipment, property and other fixed assets languishing on your books. Very often, equipment purchased years ago sits idly by, as newer equipment handles the workload of several older machines. The tendency is to hang onto these relics, thinking, "We may need these some day," or, "What could we possibly get for them?"

Bringing efficiency into an operation, however, means not having to work around equipment that has not been used for years, and probably will never be used. Unlike fine wines, used machinery and equipment rarely, if ever, get more valuable with age. Whatever you can get for unused items today is generally much more than you will realize a year or two from now. In addition, you will have the benefit of having use of that cash for that year or two. Finally, you will not be paying taxes on equipment you are no longer using, or using to its maximum. It pays to work with your employees to find out what items you no longer need, or can do without. Savings can be significant.

Shedding unused plants and other properties is something we see a lot of companies wanting to do, yet waiting for a buyer with enough cash can be a lengthy process. Purchase proposals rarely come in at the asking price—or even appraised value. After all, everyone is looking to save a few dollars wherever he can.

It is our experience that such proposals cannot be viewed in the light of purchase price alone. Instead, the entire financial picture must be considered. How long has the property been on the market? What are taxes on the property each year? Liability Insurance? Security? At the present rate, how long will it take to get a better offer (take your best guess and double it; that will be closer to actual than you think). How much money can you make on the "lower-than-acceptable" sales price if you were to put it in the bank? Or, is there something you could invest these funds in that would significantly and positively affect your bottom line? How much leaner and more focused would your organization be without this distraction? Taking these and other relevant factors into consideration, the less-than-acceptable offer you have today may be worth a lot more than you first thought.

Finally, one part of reducing working capital we did not touch on is reducing your Accounts Receivable. We believe that Revering the Customer—opening the trust relationship between you and your customers, is a two-way street. If you are providing your customers with what they want—and more—then it is their part in that trust relationship to pay their bills promptly. Nucor has a firm Net 30 day policy, and maintains a Day Sales Outstanding (DSO) of right around 30 days. John Correnti of Nucor put it this way;

> *"It is very simple, we don't borrow money from our suppliers, and we don't expect our customers to work on our money. We aren't in the banking business. If you want 60 days, go to Bethlehem or LTV!" Nucor's*

corporate policy does not allow shipment to any customer with an outstanding balance over 60 days old.

Finally, while some companies actively work their accounts receivable, beginning at the 30-day mark, others wait until the account is 90, 120 or 180 days overdue. This is much too late to do anything more than damage control. Instead, start far earlier. If the standard terms are 30 days, a follow-up call on the 31st day—inquiring if everything was satisfactory with the product or service—is certainly in order. This should be coupled with a gentle reminder that if the service or goods were indeed satisfactory, then payment according to the agreed-upon terms is expected. Your customer will be pleased that you are following up to make sure the product or service was all that it should have been. Further, he or she will recognize the reminder of payment as a memory jogger of his or her responsibility in your joint business relationship.

A far more proactive approach has been successfully employed by the credit manager of one of our clients. This credit manager makes her first call after the customer signs the credit application. In addition to letting the customer know that open credit terms have been extended, she uses the opportunity to reinforce the company's 30-day payment terms. Her second call is made 10 days after the invoice date—to ensure all materials arrived properly and inquire "if there is any reason the company cannot expect payment within its stated 30-day terms." The next call is made 25 days after invoice, to verify "the check is in the mail."

By this time, most customers come to the conclusion that it is in their best interest to pay this company promptly. We should point out that the credit manager's charm and demeanor help make each of these calls very pleasant for the customers. Yet the message is simple—she watches over open accounts very carefully; you cannot get away with "using" her money! The fact that her average DSO is in the 35-day range, while the rest of the industry is closer to the 60-day mark, is certainly a positive indicator of her success.

Aggressively managing assets is an area most companies neglect. Turbocharged Companies realize that this area of the business must be pursued as passionately as increasing sales and reducing costs. The result is improved ROAM, which translates into better cash flow and enhanced returns to shareholders—the ultimate business scorecard.

**TURBOTIP**

A strict focus on Return On Assets Managed could unlock a treasure chest of cash and profits for your business.

Checking the Mile Markers

The days of being able to run a business by the seat of your pants—if they ever existed—are certainly long gone today. While we poke a lot of fun at the "bean counters" and their obsession with numbers, we also realize that good management and financial information is essential to running a successful enterprise. You cannot wait until the end of the year to determine if you have made a profit—with that approach, you might not be in business long enough to correct the situation!

We equate good management and financial information to good health practices—you should go to your physician for periodic check-ups. This allows him/her to keep tabs on your vital signs, noting any changes and suggesting corrective or compensating action. With this practice, you should be able to stay healthy for a long and enjoyable life. If the only time you visit a doctor is after you've suffered a debilitating heart seizure, you've missed all of the benefit that years of information gathering, and acting on that information, could have given you. At that point, any thought of preventative action is moot.

Unfortunately, for most businesses, the primary management tool is the monthly financial statement. Typically, three to four weeks after the month-end, the controller produces the financial statements for the previous month. The timing normally coincides with the flurry of activity that usually surrounds trying to get everything through the business cycle before the current month ends.

Try as he might, the poor controller is rarely met with any enthusiasm. Nobody wants to pay much attention to anything he might have to say, because they are so intently focused on the current month's activities. Additionally, the information on the report is usually six and often eight weeks old. Management has a difficult time remembering the events that took place so long ago which would have affected the numbers. Workers have no better recollecting power, trying to explain why production went up or down the first three days of last month. The chorus is the same— "That was two months ago!"

Turbocharged Companies know well that monthly financial statements do have value—to accountants, auditors, bankers and shareholders. They also understand that these statements hold little real value to management in the day-to-day running of the business. They are an excellent record of a company's performance, but they are ancient history by the time they are produced. Today's business needs much more timely information than traditional monthly statements could ever produce.

Companies that tout closing their books and issuing financial reports by the tenth or seventh or even fifth day of the following month are to be commended. Yet they are still missing the mark when it comes to timely reporting of business indicators. They have decreased the lag time from six to eight weeks to four or five—a significant accomplishment. But this information is still too late to be of much use for management decisions. Monthly financial statements should be a neat, well-organized, formal confirmation of what management—and the employees—already know. This may be heresy—especially from two former accounting types—but it is true.

In order to properly manage a business, certain basic information is necessary. Further, we suggest that there are two "types" of information. The first is the more traditional "numbers" that reflects the overall performance of the organization. Nucor calls this the "Smile Report." Divisions that are achieving performance targets get a big smile stamped next to the line recording their performance. Poorly performing divisions, on the other hand, get a frown next to their numbers. To start, we suggest the following list as the absolute minimum amount of information you need about your business on a bi-weekly or monthly basis:

* Sales Revenue for every Division, Department and Product Line

* Gross Profit for every Division, Department and Product Line

* Operating Costs for every Division and Department

* Assets employed or managed by every Division, Department and Product Line

* Return on such assets by Division, Department and Product Line

Notice that we have stressed measurement by Division, Department and Product Line. All too often we find companies trying to run their businesses off a consolidated financial statement. This may tell you how the corporation as a whole is doing, but it tells you very little about how each component is doing. It does not tell you which product line is subsidizing another. It does not indicate which department is killing you with overhead. It does not tell you which division makes a lot of money but utilizes an inordinate amount of resources to accomplish that task. You must have the details to understand the significance of a move on the consolidated report—and where things can be improved.

The second type of information more closely matches the traditional "goalsetting." We call it the **Flash Report**. This type of information "translates" the more traditional business information we just reviewed into something more meaningful for the average employee. Flash Reports are regular bulletins, that contain the "what we have to do to make our company successful" barometers.

Achieving these standards results in achieving the sales, profitability and return on assets goals measured by the first set of data. In a typical Command and Control environment, such measurements would be looked on suspiciously—like "big brother" is watching. Yet in a Turbocharged Company atmosphere, where People Power has been Unleashed, such information is welcomed. Employees now understand not only the reason for the measurements, but what they mean to the company's goals and objectives. They understand how what they do impacts their fellow employee and the company as a whole.

This second type of information should be gathered and disseminated on a daily, or at least weekly, basis. It should be communicated to all employees at all levels within the appropriate division, business unit or department, as the case may be, unless competitive situations or legal requirements mandate otherwise. It needs to be ready as early in the day as possible, reporting the results of yesterday's work effort. The earlier it comes out, the greater the impact it can have on today's work. While every business is somewhat different, and the information must be tailored to its circumstances, this information could include:

* Value and quantity of quotes issued, orders received and orders shipped

* Value of total order backlog

* Value and number of purchase orders issued, and price variances experienced

* Inventory levels and turns

* Equipment and asset utilization

* Value of goods produced

* Production efficiency, downtime, rework, scrap, customer returns and machine set-up times

* On-time delivery performance

* Manpower levels, wages paid, overtime, vacation, holidays and attendance performance

* Safety incidents, injuries

* Cash receipts, accounts receivable collections

* Bank balances and dollars available under credit lines

* Updated revenue and profit projections

If some of this data is too sensitive to be released in its pure form, the data can be represented in ways that would be of little value to anyone outside the organization. Numbers can be presented in graph form, indicating the trend without disclosing actual numbers, for example. Or they could be presented as an "index," which shows movement against an unpublicized base point.

The information to be included in the Flash Report should be selected judiciously. Only "key success indicators" should be reported—those essential pieces of information necessary for people to perform tasks and focus on improvement. If the information cannot fit on a single 8-1/2" x 11" sheet of paper, you have probably included data that is not key to the success of that operation. Each division, business unit or plant should carefully review the key success indicators critical to its Flash Report.

With both types of information, not only should actual results be posted, but also what your plan requires in each area to make the company's goals. Further, this data should have direct relevance to the numbers used in the "Gainsharing Plans," which was reviewed in the First Foundation. Employees must be able to look at the Flash Report and immediately understand how the company is doing in relation to its goals. Further, they must be able to estimate accurately the impact of current performance numbers on their gainsharing payout.

Care should be taken to ensure that the information on the Flash Report, Gainsharing Plans and the company's regular financial reports all emanate from the same data base. If this is not done, there is a real possibility of conflict between the various data bases, with the attendant confusion. With a single data base, the possibility of multiple "information sources" throughout the organization is eliminated.

Armed with this kind of information, employees will not only feel trusted—they will then have the mileposts to know where they are, how far they have gone and how far they need to go. Now the curtain is lifted, and the fruits of empowerment can blossom and bloom. Now the inefficiencies stick out like the proverbial sore thumb, and the teams can focus their attention on those problems.

With the competitive nature of human beings, the simple act of measuring performance stimulates improvement. As Moira Lardakis, Progressive Corporation's Ohio Division President puts it, "what gets measured gets done." And, in fact, not only will they be done—in almost every situation, *what gets measured, gets improved!* When measurement is coupled with Gainsharing Plans, "regular" employees become entrepreneurs—dedicated to finding ways to do things better, faster and more efficiently.

Measurement is to productivity what a stop-watch is to a mile runner. Measurement is an essential ingredient to let the participant know where he or she is. In sports as in business, they are guideposts along the way.

Relentlessly Pursuing Productivity is only possible when you have vital indicators to tell you where the problems are, when you can effectively gauge the success of new ideas, and when the information you are utilizing is "real time" data. Timely, accurate and relevant information is critical to the success of any enterprise.

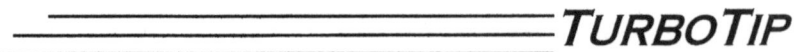

TURBOTIP

Productivity does not happen by itself—it must be squeezed out, through careful measurement and constant re-evaluation.

Staying Thin is a Full-Time Job

If you ask any dieter, he or she will tell you that the absolute worst thing about a diet is not losing the weight—it is knowing you will have to do it all over again when the weight comes back. And that yo-yo cycle of putting weight on, taking it off and putting it back on again is often times much more stressful on the body than carrying the extra pounds! That is why diet programs today focus on life-style changes—changing eating habits—to keep the weight off.

In a meeting of 400 key managers, Chrysler Chairman and CEO Robert Eaton entertained his audience with eight quotations about Chrysler's dramatic recovery. Each sounded as though it had come from that day's press clippings, yet Eaton revealed that the first was penned in 1952, the last in 1983. "We have to quit getting sick," summed up the point Mr. Eaton was trying to make.[53]

While some argue that Chrysler's mid-1990s recovery looks the same as other recoveries, there are substantial differences. First, and foremost, Chrysler makes money on each car it sells— an average profit of $1,000, rising to $7,000 on the Jeep Grand Cherokee. This is a significant departure from other carmakers who rely on other divisions for much of the income they post. Secondly, Chrysler is more focused than before, not wasting its profits on unrelated businesses. Finally, Chrysler's rapid deployment of new models makes it less dependent on the sales of a single product.[54]

Chrysler learned that to keep the weight off, old habits must change. Yet it is so very easy for companies to put that weight back on. Staff levels, once painfully cut, have a habit of slowly increasing to pre-cut levels and beyond. The process re-engineering that brought about so many good changes can easily become yesterday's task, checked off the list as accomplished and put aside.

Turbocharged Companies know that to remain leaders, they must never stop. They must never stop discovering new and better ways to do things—never stop asking why each time additional increases in overhead are proposed. Never stop asking how the company can serve its customers even better than it does today. That's what staying "thin" in the corporate world is all about.

Relentlessly Pursuing Productivity means never stopping the search for ways to do things better. There is no "slide" into complacency. Once obsolete ideas are discarded, they are never allowed to reenter your company. Progress is measured in the forward direction only—searching for ways to increase productivity, implementing it, then starting the search all over again. That's the way corporations stay thin—and maintain their low-cost competitive advantage.

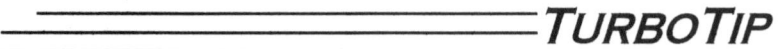 *TURBOTIP*

It is never enough to pursue productivity on a one-time basis. It must instead become a lifelong passion.

Be a Leaner, Not Meaner, Machine

The Relentless Pursuit of Productivity will clearly result in changes to your organization—changes that will result in doing a lot more with a lot less. As many companies have learned, there are several ways to approach this. One will result in a much stronger business, the other can devastate a business.

Turbocharged Companies are very aware of the significant emotional and psychological cost of "cutting heads." They do not cut heads solely for the sake of cutting, or to achieve any short-term goals. Instead, the focus is on productivity.

Cutting people merely to achieve bottom-line results, seldom achieves any significant long-term benefit. While excess "fat" must be eliminated in any organization, cutting into the "muscle and bone" of an organization can seriously endanger a company. "Belt-tightening," without any corresponding improvements in methods or productivity will seldom result in a better organization. Conversely, as companies find newer and better ways to do things, they just do not need as many people.

When cuts are necessary, your concerns, like that of the Turbocharged Companies, must be twofold. First, and most obvious, are the concerns of the employee being laid off. The use of outplacement, generous severance and other assistance will help make the experience as painless as possible, given the circumstances. Second, the remaining employees will be watching, to see how the company deals with redundant employees. The way this is done sends a very loud and clear message to those who are staying, and often has a material impact on how they perceive management and the company as a whole. Peter Lewis of Progressive Corporation puts it this way, "You have to lay off people within the context of how it will affect the people remaining in the organization."

Leaner organizations are obviously asking their people to do a lot more. The employees who have been able to retain their jobs often have to pick up some of the workload of former colleagues. While employees will work harder to help out, there is also a limited number of hours in a day. In addition to streamlining work processes and procedures, many companies are providing additional services to assist their employees. These include on-site day care, laundries, food stores and bakeries.

Sensitivity to employees' needs, when companies find it necessary to scale back employment, will help keep morale high, and customer-caring attitudes sharp.

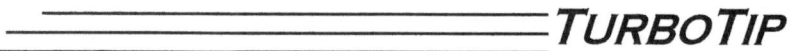

TURBOTIP

Businesses must be sensitive to the feelings and needs of all employees—those that are part of the future company, and those for whom a future role cannot be justified.

Paranoia is a Good Thing—Isn't it?

When Herb Kelleher and Rollin King formed their low-cost, shorthaul airline to shuttle people across Texas, the then dominant carriers were none too pleased, to say the least. Despite having received approval from the Texas Aeronautics Commission, rivals Braniff International and Texas International filed suit claiming the market could not support another carrier. When a trip through the Texas courts, including the Supreme Court of Texas, failed to prove them right, Braniff and Texas International appealed to the United States Supreme Court. Southwest's rivals lost that one as well.

Following the legal and administrative challenges, those same competitors launched relentless fare and advertising wars against the fledgling Southwest. "If they had just left us alone, we would have been out of business in a few years," relates Southwest's Executive Vice President of Customers, Colleen Barrett. "Instead, the more they fought and challenged us, the more our people got their backs up. It is our competitors that gave us the warrior spirit and the pride we have today. We didn't do it."

"Southwest went to the U. S. Supreme Court on two separate occasions on the right to continue to stay at Dallas Love Field. When Herb (Kelleher, Chairman & CEO) walked into the court building in Washington, D.C. to file our brief, the clerk of court looked at the brief and said, 'Are they picking on you guys again?' Hearing this comment," Ms. Barrett continued, "Herb knew that public support would, in the end, help win the airline's battles."

Wal-Mart was a rising star of the late '80s and early '90s . Under the direction of Chairman Sam Walton, the company, in 1992, overtook its rival and mentor Kmart in sales, having already surpassed it in profit a number of years before. Yet today, Wal-Mart seems to be having difficulty maintaining the momentum established by its legendary founder. Now, with diversionary difficulties blurring its customer service focus, and basking in the rays of business success, one cannot help but wonder if the company will be able to maintain its retailing leadership position. Will it continue in the ways that made it great? Or will it fall victim to its own success?

The temptation is to survey the battlefield, strewn with the carcasses of competitors who fought the hard fight and lost, and bask in that glory. Yet if history tells us anything, it tells us that the marketplace and competitors are always changing. Hippocrates wrote, "Time is that wherein there is opportunity, and opportunity is that wherein there is no great time." Today's leaders must remain constantly vigilant against the pressures of competitive forces trying to unseat them.

"It is essential to maintain a keen edge," states Southwest's Colleen Barrett. "If things are running too smoothly, we sometimes remind our employees of our competitive battles to maintain their underdog spirit." Turbocharged Companies find it vitally important to keep the organization focused on continuous improvement.

Instill in your organization the paranoia that someone else is gaining fast. Someone is making strides in product development, in productivity and in cost reduction that will outshine even yours. For in reality, there probably is—you just may not be aware of it. Charged with this sense of suspense, your employees will continue pressing for breakthroughs in productivity. The fighting spirit will continue to thrive in your organization. The business will stay razor honed. As John Correnti, President of Nucor, states, "You want to hear the footsteps of your competitors and feel their breath on the back of your neck. That's what keeps you nimble!"

Progressive Insurance takes this one step further. It deliberately hires overachievers, because they have something to prove to the world. This practice helps them avoid complacency.

In far too many companies, the comfort of complacency is all too real, once the initial productivity and cost reduction hurdles have been cleared. If a company basks in the sunlight of success, it gives competitors time to overtake it, reducing its gain to a footnote in business history. But as any runner will tell you, clearing the first few hurdles is only the start of the race. New methods and processes for doing things spring forth almost every day. Customers' needs change almost as quickly. In order to be the low-cost producer, in order to Relentlessly Pursue Productivity, it is essential never to believe you have reached your goal. Your organization must always be reaching, striving, questioning. For the minute you allow yourself to believe you have arrived at your goal, you start losing your low-cost producer edge.

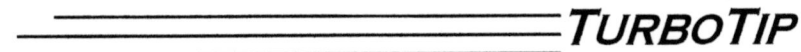 **TURBOTIP**

While it is important to enjoy your success, it pays to live with a little fear that your competitors are working hard to dethrone you.

The Lessons of Relentlessly Pursuing Productivity

Relentlessly Pursuing Productivity means endlessly searching for ways to perform better, faster, more effectively and at a lower cost, by:

Remembering hard work is not all it is cracked up to be— Look for shortcuts, smarter and easier ways to do things, and avoid errors that force you to incur costly rework.

Destroying the "Not Invented Here" syndrome—Learn from the experience of others, and focus on improving their process, rather than re-inventing them. Whenever possible, outsource non-core functions.

Watching the numbers—Ensure that you use your assets wisely and frugally; and regularly measure your performance against your prior experience, "Best Practices" and your goals.

Keeping on your toes—Staying productive requires a lifetime commitment; keep looking over your shoulder for competitors who are trying to overtake you.

Foundation Four—DOMINATE MICRONICHES

THE
TURBOCHARGED COMPANY
PROCESS

UNLEASH PEOPLE POWER

REVERE CUSTOMERS

RELENTLESSLY PURSUE PRODUCTIVITY

DOMINATE MICRONICHE

OUTPERFORM COMPETITORS

SUPERIOR RETURNS ON SHAREHOLDERS' EQUITY

The Fourth Foundation—Dominating Your MicroNiche— is only possible once your organization has Unleashed People Power, Revered its Customers and commenced the process of Relentlessly Pursuing Productivity.

Dominating Your MicroNiche—focusing on your strengths and being the best at what you do—means staking out a segment of a market niche where you can specialize, and being the "Leader of the Pack"—the best in your field. The advantages that you derive from this leadership role will provide opportunities to further Revere Your Customers and continue Pursuing Productivity. This sets up what we call the "Increasing Value Cycle"—an unbeatable competitive advantage.

Dominate?—Me??

The Fourth Foundation of a Turbocharged Company is Dominating the MicroNiche in which you compete. To understand this concept, we need to explain what a MicroNiche is, and what we mean by "dominating" it.

Traditionally, we think of competing in a market. Yet in most cases, a marketplace can be very broad. It needs some narrowing so that companies can focus their efforts on a smaller, more manageable area of the marketplace. Thus was born niche marketing, where each market is broken down into smaller markets, called niches. As customers and marketing techniques became more sophisticated, even niches proved to be too large an entity, so each niche must be broken down into what we call MicroNiches. What all this breaking down into smaller parts gives you is the ability to compete in a very well-defined field. You can then serve your customers in a particular way, without trying to be all things to all people.

That's nice for theory, but now let us describe an example of how it works in actual use. Sports equipment is a market, golf equipment is a niche and golf drivers are a MicroNiche. Callaway Golf has emerged as the dominant player in the driver MicroNiche with the introduction of its Big Bertha[i] oversized driver. Ely Callaway, Chairman and Founder of Callaway Golf, saw the frustration of both pro and duffer alike at missed drives. So, he

---

[i] Big Bertha is a registered trademark of Callaway Golf

developed Big Bertha, a totally new type of golf club—the oversized metal driver—and created his own MicroNiche. This club allows golfers to improve their accuracy, achieve longer distances and avoid mishitting the ball.

Since 1991, oversized woods have been used and endorsed by pros like Greg Norman, Fred Couples, Paul Azinger and Johnny Miller. When Ben Crenshaw, a traditionalist among golfers, won the Masters tournament in 1995 using an oversized driver (made by Cobra Golf), the last of golf's Old Guard hold-outs had been converted. Celebrities like Presidents Bill Clinton and George Bush as well as Britain's Prince Andrew all use oversized drivers. And well they should, for in their game a ball out of bounds not only brings a penalty—it could very easily hit a celebrity onlooker.[55] Callaway seized an opportunity to satisfy a customer need, and thereby created a whole new MicroNiche. Today, almost half of all American golfers use oversized woods.

The single-minded focus on this MicroNiche gave Callaway a very powerful market position. It focused all its energy and expertise in this one area, and within an extremely short period of time, Callaway became the dominant player in this MicroNiche. Prior to Callaway, no one had ever focused so much attention on this area. That focus resulted in product innovations that allowed Callaway to surge ahead of its competitors.

Rather than trying to enter the sports equipment market or the golf equipment niche, Callaway chose to zero in on the driver MicroNiche. Once Callaway had succeeded in dominating the driver MicroNiche, it used the credibility and leverage gained there to enter additional MicroNiches. First came other oversized metal woods, and then oversized irons. Using these very impressive MicroNiche strategies, Callaway has become a $550 million company in a very short period of time. Consider whether this type of growth could have been achieved had Callaway decided to enter the sports equipment market or the golf equipment niche before achieving driver MicroNiche dominance.

Southwest Airlines competes in the travel market. This includes planes, trains, busses, automobiles, ships and hot air balloons. Southwest's niche is air travel. But, Southwest has very successfully created its own MicroNiche—the market for budget-conscious, shorthaul, point-to-point travelers. In this way, it has set itself apart from other airlines that may travel greater distances, provide various levels of service or serve meals.

Progressive started by being a leader in the market for insuring higher risk drivers, and the company turned this into its own MicroNiche. Using the experience and legendary service levels developed in this demanding segment, Progressive is now taking the opportunity to enter another MicroNiche within the standard automobile insurance niche.

By focusing on MicroNiches, an organization creates simplicity of purpose—the domination of that MicroNiche. All energies are devoted to producing a better product, offering a better service, and responding to customer needs. Employees are not distracted by competing or conflicting priorities. They know what their task is, and they are focused on it alone.

Sometimes, if a current MicroNiche has been exhausted—or conquered—a company may have to go to another MicroNiche. The company continues serving its present MicroNiche while using the experiences gained in the first to begin work in a second MicroNiche. With this strategy, companies can continue moving into one MicroNiche after another (see figure 3). While the focus is still on conquering MicroNiches, this strategy, applied successfully, can result in dominating most or all the MicroNiches in a niche, allowing effective control of the niche. To be sure, such niche domination is purely the result of a series of MicroNiche dominations.

A company can certainly operate successfully in several MicroNiches at the same time. This is quite true of Chrysler. It operates in the automobile market and successfully competes in—and dominates—the minivan and four wheel drive MicroNiches. Additionally, Chrysler is pursuing several other MicroNiches (*e.g.* small cars) but has yet to achieve *domination* in all of them. If, however, the pursuit of multiple MicroNiches dilutes your efforts in the first, MicroNiche Dominance could be jeopardized.

MICRONICHE STRATEGY
(Figure 3)

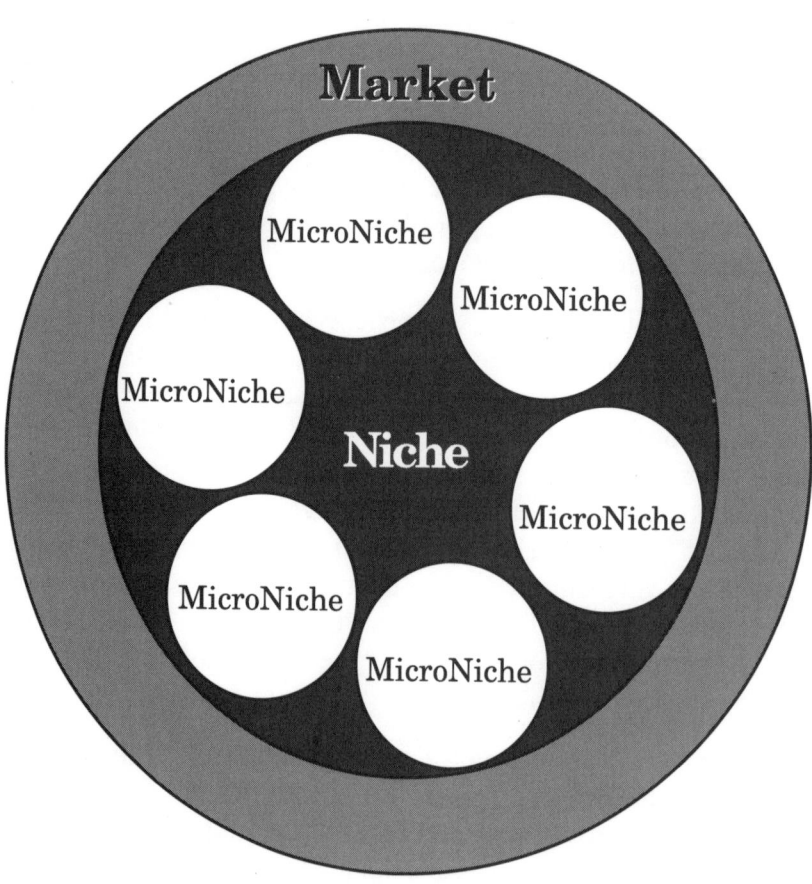

At this point, you may be wondering just what this means to your organization. You can become much more efficient as you specialize in one particular area in which to serve your customers. Your customers will quickly recognize your expertise in this area and think of you first when they need your product or service.

Now that we have reviewed MicroNiches and their importance, let's examine what we mean by dominating them. Market dominance may mean many things to many people. To some, it is being number one in the industry, by whatever criteria you select. While this may be important in some circles, it does not necessarily reflect our meaning of Dominating Your MicroNiche. "Being biggest is not all that important," states Nucor's Ken Iverson, "It's all ego." According to Chrysler's Mike Morrison, Executive Director of Corporate Communications, "We're not trying to be the number-one automaker in size. Instead, we want to be the number-one automaker in innovative design and number-one in low-cost production of quality products. That's our market dominance." Southwest Airlines, on the other hand, always strives to be the number-one carrier in each route it serves.

So how do you square all this up? We define Dominating Your MicroNiche as being in a position that allows you to control your own destiny. For Southwest, it is controlling the air routes, but it is also being the low-cost, high-productivity leader in the airlines. For Nucor, it is low-cost leadership. For Chrysler it is low-cost and high innovation. For Progressive, it is innovative marketing techniques, superior service and sensitivity to the trauma being experienced by their customers. These firms have found a way to "dominate" that permits them to exercise control over the direction their companies take. They can maintain more of a proactive stance rather than reacting to their competitors. They can be industry innovators and leaders rather than "me-too" followers. They set the pace in the industry and keep everyone else a few paces behind. Just as their competitors are beginning to adapt and respond to their last innovation, they respond with yet another. This, in our view, is Dominating Your MicroNiche.

Since 1971, Southwest Airlines has focused on low-cost, shorthaul, point-to-point, customer-focused air transportation.

Despite plenty of opportunities to diversify into other arenas, Southwest remains dedicated to serving its MicroNiche. While the rest of the airline industry, in the early to mid-1990s was drowning in a sea of red ink, Southwest was happily posting profits year after year. Instead of becoming complacent, "Kelleher's Crew" was facing stiff opposition from other carriers, trying desperately to find a way to compete with Southwest. While Continental inaugurated and closed its Continental Lite service, and other airlines tried similar moves, Southwest kept doing what it does best—treating its tightly targeted customer like royalty. Never losing sight of its mission, never succumbing to the temptation to offer classes of service, meals or long haul routes, Southwest continues to be an American success story.

Southwest has deliberately structured its organization to be able to dominate its MicroNiche and to allow it to dominate most of its routes. Everything it does is designed to lower costs and improve service—two criteria vital to this MicroNiche. All of its planes, for example, are Boeing 737s, which saves the airline from the need to train pilots on a variety of different planes and having to stock a plethora of parts for many different airframes. Its point-to-point routes eliminate the need for expensive "hubs" and dramatically facilitate faster aircraft turnaround time. Its new "ticketless travel" further reduces costs and increases customer convenience. In addition, it does not offer connections or baggage transfers to other airlines, enabling it to avoid inheriting delays and operational problems from other airlines.

These lower costs allow Southwest to offer very attractive ticket prices, which promote increased passenger traffic, which facilitates more flights. More flights per day means fixed costs can be spread over a wider base, further lowering their costs per seat mile. Couple that with the convenience that more flights per day provides passengers, and you see why MicroNiche dominance—in a variety of ways—works for Southwest, and its customers.

Dominating your hill puts you "in the driver's seat." Remember Nucor, the feisty steel maker reshaping our ideas about steel mills? Its low-cost dominance in that marketplace forces its competitors to dance to Nucor's tune. The company showed great fortitude by spending hundreds of millions of dollars to import a relatively unproven technique for making hot-rolled sheet steel. Despite overwhelming start-up problems, Nucor persisted, and the company succeeded in producing steel at significantly lower costs than its established competitors. This allowed Nucor the opportunity to adjust its pricing based on the amount of work it had. When mill time was open, it was time to cut prices. When the mills were running at full capacity, it was time to raise prices. With this elementary pricing strategy, you can appreciate how Nucor could virtually set the price of steel for the entire industry—something its competitors did not like one bit.

Interestingly, Nucor faces challenges of its own as ex-Nucor managers set up competitive steel making facilities and compete against their former company. Like Southwest's challenges by Continental, USAir and others, it will be interesting to watch the developments in the steel industry.

Progressive's innovative 1-800 call-in line, which allows consumers to get comparative quotations on auto insurance, has competitors shaking their heads. Not only will Progressive quote you its rate for your insurance needs, it will also provide the comparison rates of their three largest competitors. Progressive's rates are not always the lowest available to the consumer, but when they are, Progressive secures the business for the price of a phone call. Their competitors, many of whom make their money from investing cash rather than policy sales, have yet to catch on. They are too busy investing money to watch where the money comes from in the first place.

Truly Dominating a MicroNiche is only possible in an organization once you have Unleashed People Power, are Revering Your Customers and are Relentlessly Pursuing Productivity. Without Unleashing People Power, you will not have really ignited the true power of your organization. If you are not Revering Your Customers, you will not be interested in satisfying—much less exceeding—their needs. Thus, you will not be in a position to want to determine your customers' needs, much less build an organization to satisfy them. Finally, if you are

201

not Relentlessly Pursuing Productivity, you will never be the low-cost producer, and you'll be "out of the game."

Relentlessly Pursuing Productivity and Revering Customers allows an organization to move toward MicroNiche Dominance. Ironically, when Dominance is achieved, it then fuels further opportunities to improve productivity, hence value to the customers. MicroNiche dominance allows an organization to Revere its Customers even more, while allowing further productivity increases. This then fuels the organization's ability to serve its customer even better. We call this the much sought-after **Increasing Value Cycle**.

The balance of this section will detail specific ways to identify and dominate your MicroNiche, and ways to stay focused. As you can see, it is very easy to have your focus blurred, so remaining keenly focused on what you do is vital to the success of your Turbocharged Company.

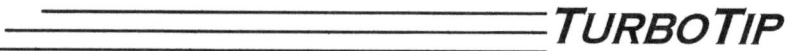

TURBOTIP

Pick a pond where you can be the "biggest" fish—and don't jump to another pond until you have gobbled up all the fish in the first pond.

Determine Your Strengths and Weaknesses

In order to determine the MicroNiche in which to compete—
or create—it is vital to know what your organization is good at.
Organizations can typically do a lot of different things, but it is
focusing on what you do best—and sticking to just that—that will
pay rich rewards in terms of Dominating your MicroNiche.

For your business to transform itself into a Turbocharged
Company, it must determine its core competencies. This will start
you in the direction of defining your MicroNiche. And be specific
here—Southwest is not in the transportation business, it is not in
the airline business, it isn't even in the "We'll take you to Hawaii,
Europe or Rio" business. It is in the low-cost, shorthaul, point-
to-point commuter business. Southwest knows what it does well,
and it focuses on just that.

American Paper Group, Ltd. in tiny Boardman, Ohio is the
largest maker of one particular type of envelope in the world—
and not many people have ever heard of the company! It doesn't
make envelopes anywhere near the scale of a Westvaco, or a
Scott Paper or an International Paper. This comparatively tiny
$40 million firm is, however, the world's leading manufacturer of
church collection envelopes. With more than 350,000 churches in
the United States, two-thirds of which use collection envelopes,
the company has carved out a rather nice MicroNiche for itself.[56]

MBNA, the Delaware-based affinity credit card bank, could obviously expand into traditional banking functions. Yet it has no retail facilities, nor does it seem to have any plans to create them. Its strength, hence its MicroNiche, is providing a high level of service to a very select group of upscale consumers through affinity-based credit cards. Its target audiences are professional societies, college alumni associations and other upscale membership organizations. By carefully targeting its customer, MBNA is able to boast of having the most affluent customer base in the credit card industry. That means more use of the company's credit card and fewer write-offs for bad debt.[57]

As companies continue to discover, focusing on what you do best is the only way to succeed in business long term. Kodak's CEO George Fisher has refocused the organization on its core strength—imaging. Shedding some $7.9 billion in non-imaging divisions, including the large Sterling-Winthrop drug unit, Mr. Fisher was able to reduce some of Kodak's debt, allowing it more flexibility in months and years to come.[58] Note particularly here that Kodak focused on the imaging market. This is important as Kodak's original market—photographic film—is rapidly headed for the endangered species list. Thus Kodak redefined its core competency to that of imaging and focused the talents of the organization in that area

The lesson is clear: A company should focus on what it does best and get rid of all other distractions that prevent it from serving the needs of its customers.

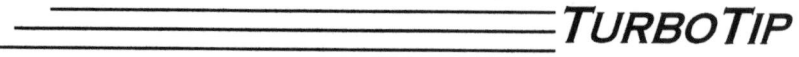

TURBOTIP

Build on your real strengths rather than on what you would like them to be.

Build Your MicroNiche Around Your Customer

The next step in the process of Dominating your MicroNiche is determining exactly what your customer wants. If you are in the scaffolding supply business and want to focus on scaffolding for erecting refinery tanks, then it is time to talk to oil companies, both major and specialty, to find out what they want, expect and would ideally love in a scaffolding supplier. Talk to tank erecting contractors and tank maintenance contractors. Get inside their heads to determine their "hot buttons." Price is a consideration, no doubt, but there is always so much more. Maybe the manner in which the scaffolding is erected, or the particular type of scaffolding, or the quick assembly and disassembly are as important to the customer as price—perhaps even more important. Find out what would make their job easier, safer or more productive. Then go back and fashion your organization to provide those customers with what they want. The key is—give your customers what they expect—and more.

Robert Eaton, Chrysler's Chairman, learned this lesson the hard way when the J. D. Power and Associates Initial Quality Study results came out in late May 1994. Chrysler's quality ratings, despite a considerable focus on quality, had actually gotten worse since the last report had been issued. In a hastily called meeting of executives, Eaton discovered the reason for the drop in ratings. Although the vehicles had passed all their internal quality tests, those standards were based on meeting Chrysler's engineering specifications. And true to that focus, the company had the lowest warranty costs among the Big Three. But the Powers study focused not only on technical quality, but also on the *customer's perception* of quality. Under that standard, the placement or number of cupholders, and the ease of getting into and out of the vehicle are as important as fit, finish and mechanical performance. And those were quality standards Chrysler people were not adequately measuring.[59] Their quality effort had been focused on the wrong customer—engineering specifications do not buy cars, customers do. The lesson has had a significant impact on Chrysler's new product development efforts from that point on.

Some of Chrysler's competitors completely missed this point when trying to gain minivan market share. Instead of primarily focusing on the marketplace to determine the consumers' needs and expectations, they spent a lot of time studying other carmakers. Chrysler, the pre-eminent leader of the minivan market, became the major part of this market research. Competitive products were designed, produced and introduced to compete directly with Chrysler's existing vehicles. The trouble was, Chrysler completely redesigned its minivans. The 1996 Chrysler was a major advance in this product category.[60] Features like heaters for the front and rear windshield wipers that melt away ice and snow, cupholders that even hold a Big Gulp®[i] soft drink cup, sliding doors on the driver's side, individual temperature controls for both front passengers and safety standards exceeding 1998 requirements overwhelmingly pleased consumers.

As the leader in the minivan MicroNiche, Chrysler was able to focus its energies on innovations that would enhance value and customer satisfaction. Followers in the market are often distracted trying to catch the leader; as a result, they divert some of their focus from the ultimate customer's needs.

Reading newspapers, industry trade journals or marketing position reports will never substitute for face to face contact with

---

[i] Big Gulp® is a registered trademark of The Southland Corporation

your customers—in their environment—talking about what they need, what their frustrations are and what would make their lives easier. By the time this kind of information is published, it is aged. It may no longer even be relevant. The Ivory Tower Syndrome has doomed more companies than anyone could ever imagine.

Armed with your organization's core competencies—and a thorough understanding of what your customers demand, would like and would leap for joy over—enables you to move closer to defining your MicroNiche.

TURBOTIP

The needs of customers must be your highest priority in designing your MicroNiche.

Never Play on a Level Field!

"Having a competitive advantage in a business is about as important as having a gun in a knife fight!"

— Gary Barron, Exec. VP, Chief Operations Officer, Southwest Airlines

A competitive advantage sets your company's product or service apart from your competition. It provides a reason for your customer to want your product or service over any competitor's. Why, for example, in a field of hamburger chains, would you prefer a Wendy's[i] over a McDonalds'[ii]—or a McDonalds' over a Burger King?[iii] Perhaps you prefer Wendy's fresh cooked over McDonalds' fast service—or McDonalds' fast service over Burger King's flame broiled. In the end, they are all cooked ground beef on a bun, but if you specifically want fresh, or flame broiled, or special sauce, then only one brand will do.

Even more important than having a competitive advantage is getting customers to recognize and prefer those products. If all you want is a hamburger with fries and a shake, then you are looking for a basic commodity—food—and virtually any fast food chain will fill your needs. If, however, you have a taste for a

---

[i] Wendy's is a registered trademark of Wendy's International, Inc.

[ii] McDonalds is a registered trademark of McDonald's Corporation

[iii] Burger King is a registered trademark of Burger King Corporation

particular double meat burger with a unique sauce and other fine features, then competitive advantages come into play, and only one restaurant is going to get your business.

Probably the strongest competitive advantage any company can have is its people. Earnie Deavenport of Eastman Chemical Company states, "The only real sustainable competitive advantage of any company, including Eastman, is the ability to unlock the potential of [its employees'] mind and spirit."[61]

One of the most prevalent advantages today is cost leadership. Companies with the lowest cost structure, coupled with the quality and service the customer wants, have a significant advantage over any competitor. It allows you to set your price to capture a fair profit while providing ultimate value to your customer. Chrysler's low-cost leadership allows it to pass along its savings to consumers as value enhancements—they get more for their money.

Nucor enjoys the same competitive advantage. It has been able to price its steel in the market knowing its worker productivity is higher than anyone else in the industry, hence its costs are lower. Essentially, Nucor captured all the business it needed to keep its plants running at full tilt, and its competitors fought over what was left. Talk about an enviable position![62]

Nucor has taken a lot of heat concerning the $150 million it has invested in an iron carbide plant it is building in Trinidad. When this plant is on-line, it will reduce Nucor's reliance on traditional scrap materials, which are becoming increasingly more difficult—and more expensive—to buy. Vice President and General Manager of Nucor's Crawfordsville, Indiana plant, Larry Roos, explains, "Nucor is not afraid to take risks. While the plant has had some problems, it could give us a big competitive advantage in years to come."

In today's highly competitive environment, having a cost advantage is a definite plus. But this is by no means the only competitive advantage a company can have. Maytag appliances have often cost more than their competitors, but their quality is second to none. Many consumers have determined that there is a competitive advantage to this level of quality, and they are willing to pay a little extra for it.

Superior service can be a competitive advantage. In addition to Southwest Airlines, Nordstrom's and Wal-Mart have used their well-known customer-caring service as a competitive advantage. Technology can be a competitive advantage—a concept Microsoft Corporation knows well with its Disk Operating Software (MS-DOS[i]). Patents can be a competitive advantage, and pharmaceutical companies use this concept to great benefit. In short, anything that gives you an edge over your competition is a competitive advantage. It helps differentiate your product or service from the "rest of the pack."

Pepsi,[ii] seeking a competitive advantage over rival Coke[iii] in the spring of 1994, began test labeling Diet Pepsi with an expiration date. The concept focused on the little-known fact that aspartame, or NutraSweet®,[iv] loses its sweetness after two to three months. It was a risky strategy, but one that worked well as Pepsi, at least for a while, found a way to set itself apart from the competition. Freshness of product became the selling point.[63]

Competitive advantages are important as long as your competitors do not have them, and your customers still want them. Frequent Flyer packages were a competitive advantage to the first airline that had them. Now, they are the price of entry in the airline business. They essentially have become a commodity, losing any competitive advantage they once had.

Similarly, if the competitive advantage you can offer no longer matters to your customer, it has ceased to be of value. Consider Sony's Betamax versus VHS video. Clearly Betamax had superior color, clarity and technology over the VHS format, but VHS machines were cheaper to produce, and the quality level was acceptable to a consumer who had just moved from TV antennas

---

[i] MS-DOS is a registered trademark of Microsoft Corporation

[ii] Pepsi and Diet Pepsi are registered trademarks of the Pepsi-Cola Bottling Company

[iii] Coke is the registered trademark of the Coca-Cola Bottling Company

[iv] NutraSweet® is a registered trademark of the NutraSweet Company

to cable. As more and more consumers began to focus their purchases on VHS, more manufacturers started producing VHS machines and more tapes became available. Though technologically superior, the Beta system was soon all but forgotten in the video market.

The way to get a competitive advantage is to listen to your customer. Determine what the customer would like, given what you are uniquely positioned to offer. Put yourself in your customer's place and ask yourself a simple question, "Why should I buy your product or service in the face of all the other products and services similar to it?"

If you can answer this question by meeting a unique and distinct need, want or desire of your customer, you have a competitive advantage. If you cannot answer this question, you have more work to do. Without one or more sustainable competitive advantages, most businesses will find it difficult to survive, much less outperform competitors.

When you have been able to identify a market segment that allows you to utilize your company's strengths and core competencies—one in which you are able to satisfy the unique needs of your customers, and one in which you have valuable advantages your competitors do not have—then you are closing in on identifying your MicroNiche.

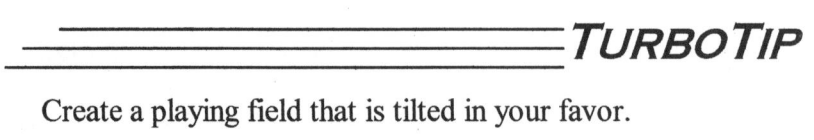

Create a playing field that is tilted in your favor.

Is Your MicroNiche Worthwhile?

Even when you have determined a market segment within your core competency—one that allows you to satisfy your customers while providing a distinct advantage over your competitors—you cannot yet be sure this is the correct MicroNiche for your company. A final step must be undertaken. You must determine if the MicroNiche is worthwhile. It is of little value to dominate a market segment that is rapidly declining, overburdened with problems or just plain unprofitable.

The last buggy whip manufacturer in this country truly dominated that market. He stayed in that business until he had all the market share there was. But it was all for naught, for within a few years of dominating that market, it disappeared. The horseless buggy did not require a whip.

Turbocharged Companies keep their eyes and ears open to continuing developments in the marketplace. Are new materials and processes replacing today's technology? Are changes within the marketplace making your product or service obsolete? Have the customers' demands, needs or expectations changed? Continuously evaluating the viability of your product or service in the face of changing technology and customer needs has to become second nature. Had Kodak not looked around and embraced electronic imaging, doubtless it would not be in the position it is today. Kodak might have owned a segment, but it would have had a limited future. But because George Fisher, Kodak's Chairman, could step back and see where the company was headed, adjustments could be made, which should enable Kodak to continue well into the next century.

To be sure, it is not essential for a market segment to be in a "high-growth" mode in order for it to be worthwhile. If you have distinct advantages over your competitors, it is quite feasible to be very successful at dominating a stable, yet low-growth market. Obviously, low-growth market segments will, at some point, place restrictions on your company's ability to expand.

What do you do if you are thinking, "I'm not sure my MicroNiche is worthwhile. The market we compete in is dying. What do I do?" Our recommendation is to continue dominating the MicroNiche you are in, but begin the process of re-examining your company to determine in which other MicroNiches you could compete. Position yourself so that you milk the present MicroNiche for all you can, then make the shift to your new MicroNiche on your timetable, not someone else's.

The lesson is clear—keep your eyes open for those "outside influences" that could drastically change your MicroNiche and its position in the marketplace. Pursuing a MicroNiche that will not provide long-term profitability is wasted effort. That long-term profitability might be affected by a segment that is declining, or because competitive pressures make it impossible to make money in that MicroNiche. Keep in contact with your customers, and with your industry. Do not allow your organization to operate in an information vacuum. If the viability of your MicroNiche is threatened, re-examine your strengths, review the needs of your customers and make the necessary changes in your organization to create or compete in a new MicroNiche.

If, however, you operate in or have identified a market segment:

* that allows your company to use its core
   competencies,

* that allows you to satisfy the unique needs of your
   customers,

* in which you have distinct advantages over your competition,

* and that you have determined to be worthwhile,

then MicroNiche Domination—and all the benefits it brings—is now a tangible reality for your company.

TURBOTIP

Look for an alternate route if your business is headed toward the proverbial brick wall.

Buy Everyone Blinders!

Once you have determined your MicroNiche, it's time to put on blinders. No, not the kind of blinders that would prevent the company from seeing what is going on in the marketplace. Not the kind of blinders that enable the front line troops—those employees who have day-to-day contact with your customers—from noticing new customer trends, ideas and suggestions. But blinders that keep the organization focused on its sole purpose—serving the customers' needs in the MicroNiche in which you compete, or are creating.

A company cannot be all things to all customers. Chameleons may work well in nature and politics, but they have no place in business. Turbocharged Companies have learned that focusing—laser focusing—on their MicroNiche is the only way to successfully compete in and Dominate their MicroNiche.

In the absence of good, clear communication and direction, it is very easy for employees to lose focus. If you are concerned that this is happening in your company, ask your colleagues. Ask them to tell you, in their own words, the specific mission of the company. Ask if they can define the target customer. Colleen Barrett of Southwest Airlines is proud to note that all Southwest's employees, regardless of rank or seniority, are keenly aware of the mission and focus of the company. She reasons that if everyone knows why the airline is in business, the organization will be able to devote all its time and attention to serving its customers. There will not be distractions, false starts and other frustrating diversions.

If, in your research, you get more than one answer, the mission and target customer of your company is not understood. If you get as many variations as you have respondents, your organization is really unfocused, and needs help—fast! Businesses should not delay in taking the steps to communicate their vision and MicroNiche to every employee—to ensure they stay focused on just that. With this attitude, you will rapidly move closer to MicroNiche Dominance.

Just as important as keeping employees focused on the mission of the organization, is keeping the corporation focused on that mission as well. Anything that distracts the organization, in part or in whole, from serving the needs of its customer—thus dominating its MicroNiche—is a threat to the organization. The Kmart story has been all too well documented in business journals and investor guides. The nation's number-one retailer, having blown past longtime leader Sears, Roebuck & Company, was unceremoniously dumped from the top spot by rival Wal-Mart.

Scrape away all the rhetoric, and you will find that the real story here is one of focus. Sears began in business decades before its discount store rivals. It had plenty of time to refine its operations, sharpen its focus. Instead, it began diversifying. First it established Allstate Insurance Company, then Homart Development (a developer of shopping centers). During the 1980s, diversification really took off. In short order, Sears purchased Dean Witter Reynolds (stocks) and Coldwell Banker & Co. (real estate), while starting up the Discover Card, Prodigy and Advantis programs.

By 1994, the retailer was forced to take drastic action to refocus itself. Allstate, Dean Witter (including Discover Card Operations), Coldwell Banker, and the retailer's legendary catalog division were either sold off or closed. Sears was also actively trying to unload Homart Development and return to the retailing roots from which it came.[64]

It is not hard to conclude that all this loading and unloading of diversified companies took the organization's eyes away from its core retailing business and plummeted it to third place in that segment. And we cannot help wondering if Sears, having won its long-fought battle with Montgomery Ward for retail supremacy, simply lulled itself into complacency, ignoring the very real threat from Kmart.[65]

Kmart, started in 1962, focused on discount retailing as its strategy to compete with Sears. To its undoing, Sears did not appear to take this threat very seriously. Kmart grew, undeterred by Sears, until, in 1990, its sales revenue surpassed the lethargic giant to claim the number-one retailing spot.

Yet even as it was reaching for top spot, Kmart was basking in its own success. It decided, in the early 1980s, to change directions. It opened two cafeteria locations and the Designer Depot chain of off-price clothing stores. Both ventures were sold in 1986. The buying binge then started in earnest with the addition of Makro warehouse stores, Pay Less Drug Stores and PACE membership warehouse stores. All were purged from the corporate family by the end of 1993, with the sale of the PACE warehouses to rival Wal-Mart.

Thin once again, the nation's number-one retailer forayed into purchases of The Sports Authority (sporting goods), Office Max (discount office supply), Builder's Square (home improvement), Borders and Waldenbooks (books), plus 13 department stores in the Czech Republic.[66] In the meantime, rival Wal-Mart had smoothly moved past Kmart, stealing the top spot held but briefly by Kmart.

By the end of the first quarter of 1995, Kmart had shed its majority stake in both The Sports Authority and Office Max, agreed to sell off the Pay Less Drug Store chain, and replaced longtime employee, President and CEO Joseph Antonini. Further planned divestitures will leave the company once again focused on its core business—discount retailing. In the meantime, however, largely ignored Sears is strengthening its position, nearing Kmart in sales in early 1995 results.[67]

Wal-Mart, in contrast, though starting out the same year as Kmart, has remained fairly well-focused on discount general merchandise retailing—at least until recently. Previous corporate additions were added to strengthen Wal-Mart's distribution network, far and away superior to anyone else's in the industry. We see, however, the addition of the Sam's Club and the PACE warehouse chain (purchased from rival Kmart)—coupled with Wal-Mart's entry into the Mexican market—as a distraction to Wal-Mart's core business. Troubles in these areas may cause the corporation to lose focus. The company reported same store sales declines at the combined Sam's Club/PACE warehouses during 1994, while noting industry concern over the warehouse club concept. Further, Wal-Mart's entry into the Mexican market has been less than successful as the U. S. formula is adjusted to the Mexican way of doing business. While a global perspective may be important, we cannot help wondering if Wal-Mart stores, still adjusting to life after Sam Walton, will suffer from this distraction.

The lesson is elementary—Turbocharged Companies stick to what they do best. They are not interested in building the world's largest office building, nor are they trying to cover a broad spectrum. They stay very focused on their MicroNiches. As old and as simple as that concept is, many organizations, "feeling their oats," pursue other strategies—often with disastrous long-term results.

Put the blinders on your organization. Keep everyone focused on enhancing your strengths, satisfying your customer's needs, building your competitive advantages and being the leader of your MicroNiche.

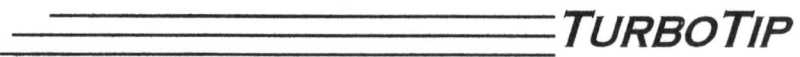

TURBOTIP

Dominating Your MicroNiche is one circumstance where being single-minded could result in admiration—and success.

Resist Those Greener Pastures

Most business owners are, by nature, optimists. If they were not, they would still be working for someone else. After all, the cold reality is that success seldom comes easily in the very competitive environment in which we operate. Most people have to work very hard to achieve their dreams.

Yet being an optimist can sometimes work against you in business. It often causes you to chart aggressive forecasts or goals for your business. All too often, though, the actual results fall short of the lofty goals. If the target is missed by a small margin, the business owner will probably be reasonably happy and try to make up the shortfall in the next business period. If the target is missed by a large margin, or if the business person is constantly trying to play "catch-up," then disenchantment sets in. He or she reasons that the product line, the business or the segment he is in is not really all that attractive. So he begins to covet another.

An entrepreneur started a small chain of retail gasoline stations. Within a few years, he had built the business up to 20 locations but, to his disappointment, the business never made any significant profit. After a decade of seemingly lackluster performance, the entrepreneur contracted the dreaded "Grass is Greener" syndrome. He concluded that there never was any future in the retail gasoline business, and that the wholesale gasoline business would be much better.

Well, before you knew it, the entrepreneur was knee-deep in the wholesale gasoline business. Like most start-up businesses, things did not go quite according to plan here either. By this time, the entrepreneur had made an important discovery. Though both businesses involved gasoline, that was about the only thing that they had in common. The customers were obviously different, as were their needs. The service each required was vastly different. And cash flow was dramatically different. While retail customers paid immediately by cash or credit card, wholesale customers expected generous credit terms—and did not always stick to them. The largest surprise was profit margin. The entrepreneur knew margins were thin in the retail gasoline business, but those margins were huge compared to the wholesaler's margins.

The entrepreneur's fortunes continued to decline. He was spending most of his time and cash trying to stabilize the wholesale business. Thinking that securing large supply contracts was the answer, he submitted and won several large bids. But, due to equipment and other problems, he was unable to make all the delivery schedules. This enabled his customers to invoke penalty clauses that had been specified in the bid documents. He soon discovered that an irate wholesale customer has a lot more teeth than an irate retail customer—and does not hesitate to use them.

With attention and cash resources diverted to the wholesale business, the retail chain began to suffer. The physical appearance of the stations deteriorated, as regular maintenance had been scaled back to conserve cash. Employee morale plummeted, resulting in the loss of several excellent people. Finally, revenues began to decline.

The entrepreneur wound up losing both businesses—a fate he might have avoided had he not fallen prey to the "Grass is Greener" syndrome. He could have lessened the impact of the syndrome by selling off or liquidating the retail gasoline chain before entering the wholesale business. Instead, he chose to do both. In the process, he diverted the precious little cash flow the retail business provided into the enormous expense of setting up the wholesale unit.

Instead, a much wiser decision would have been to stay in the original retail gasoline business and find ways to make it more profitable. That was a business he knew, had experience in and could "get his arms around." Many other entrepreneurs in this industry had found ways to increase sales, maximize efficiency and generate profits. Had he invested his energies into transforming his chain into a Turbocharged Company, his fortune might have turned out quite differently.

No matter what your business, or position within it, the "Grass is Greener" syndrome hits everyone at some point in time. The trick is to take the antidote—reality—and stick to your vision before the syndrome has a chance to work. Every enterprise has its problems. There is not a business today that does not have competitors, continual pressure on margins and the need to remain intensely innovative. Regardless of how good some other business appears, chances are it is not that great. Any business is still going to take a lot of work, time, energy and resources.

We encourage companies to examine their own "bird in the hand" carefully before taking any actions to diversify. Often, it is management's familiarity with the company, the customers and the challenges that mask the vision of the diamond-in-the-rough it is holding. Those same elements also mask the downside of the enticing opportunities that lie on the other side of the fence.

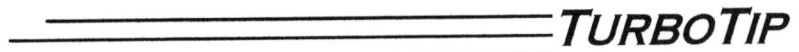

TURBOTIP

Dedicated persistence to the business you are in will generally yield greater rewards than will coveting another.

The Lessons of Dominating Your MicroNiche

Dominating Your MicroNiche is accomplished by:

Determining Your Strengths and Weaknesses—What product or service you are uniquely positioned to offer your customer.

Building Your MicroNiche Around Your Customers—Determining their needs and how you can best serve them.

Never Playing on a Level Field—Build and maintain competitive advantages.

Determining if Your MicroNiche is Worthwhile—Know if it is growing, declining or possible to make money in.

Buying Everyone Blinders—Keeping the entire organization laser focused on serving the customers in your MicroNiche.

Resisting Greener Pastures—The business you have today can generally be more profitable in the long run than the business you are dreaming about.

Start Your Engines

THE
T<small>URBOCHARGED</small> C<small>OMPANY</small>
PROCESS

UNLEASH PEOPLE POWER

REVERE CUSTOMERS

RELENTLESSLY PURSUE PRODUCTIVITY

DOMINATE MICRONICHE

OUTPERFORM COMPETITORS

SUPERIOR RETURNS ON SHAREHOLDERS' EQUITY

You have now had the opportunity to review the Four Foundations and what they mean, how they interact and what they can do for your business. Now is the time to apply the knowledge you have acquired.

Here you will learn how to start this Process in your company, regardless of its size or financial condition. Practical suggestions from actual cases will guide you through this Process, to ensure your organization has the best chance of becoming a Turbocharged Company.

Decide Your Event

This section of the book is dedicated to implementing the steps necessary to transform your organization into a Turbocharged Company. First, it is important to note that implementation strategies are different, depending on the position in which your company finds itself. If your company is clearly in a crisis situation, with the threat of bankruptcy, liquidation or foreclosure in the not-too-distant future, you will want to employ the **Intensive Strategy**. Under this scenario, the implementation strategy is more condensed, more focused and aggressive. After all, you do not want to be in the position of saying, "If only I had tried . . ." when it is much too late to try anything.

Perhaps, on the other hand, your situation is "We're doing okay but need or would like to do much better." You are not losing money, but you are not making the profits that your company should. If this more closely defines your situation, the **Moderate Strategy** would be better for your organization. Here there is more time available and efforts can be focused differently. The amount of risk involved is reduced, as the aggressive measures called for in the Intensive Strategy might not be appropriate in this situation. This strategy is more evolutionary than revolutionary.

Finally, your situation may be one of "We're doing great now, but we can be doing so much better." Your company is on sound financial ground and by most standards doing well. Yet, there is a vision of the company performing much better, at an entirely different level than it is presently operating. Because the company is performing well, there might not be the need to implement the Turbocharged Company Process all at one time. A more paced introduction, our **Gradual Strategy**, may best suit the dynamics of the organization and avoid risking the very structure that brought the organization its success.

We suggest you read over all three strategies, then carefully examine your organization and decide how best to proceed. Even though your organization is doing okay, you may opt for the Intensive Strategy, due to the need to "shake up the organization" or unseat some long-entrenched corporate culture. Conversely, while you may clearly be doing well and just want to position the organization for further gains, many of the ideas presented in the first two strategies can be incorporated into your own program, dependent on the needs of your particular situation. Each company's situation is different, and this will drive its individual implementation strategy.

Whatever approach you use, go forward with the confidence that you have the power in your hands to dramatically change your organization. We have given you the principles, and we are about to give you the "how-to." With persistence and determination, and the creativity and involvement of your greatest corporate asset—you and your fellow employees, your business will be ready to commence the Process of becoming a Turbocharged Company.

IMPLEMENTATION STRATEGIES

1. Crisis situation—Intensive Strategy

2. Not in a crisis, but still underperforming—Moderate Strategy

3. Doing well, but see the opportunity to do even better—Gradual Strategy

Intensive Strategy—When the Wolves are at the Door

Your organization might be losing significant amounts of money, or might be facing some other threat to its future viability. Sales might be declining, productivity might have deteriorated, morale could be low or several key employees might have "jumped ship." Bankers could be re-examining lines of credit or may have withdrawn them altogether. Suppliers might be beginning to question the financial health of the organization. This is indicative of the classic "wolves-at-the-door" situation.

If your organization finds itself in a predicament similar to this, the Intensive Strategy outlined here is the implementation plan for you. The steps are quick, the measures decisive.

This strategy can be implemented in entire companies, or in divisions, plants, branches or stores. While we will use the term CEO, this could just as easily be replaced by Division Manager, Plant Manager, Branch Manager or Store Manager.

Abandon Command and Control

In this situation, the first step is to abandon Command and Control management immediately, if it is still prevalent. The old "employees should just work and keep quiet" attitude of management must, at last, be escorted to the front gates. The first casualty must be the end of management "perks." The maintenance people must be asked to remove the reserved parking signs. Executive dining rooms, first-class travel, country-club memberships and all the other "trappings" of senior management must go. These suffocating symbols of the past must give way to the fresh, clear ideas of Unleashed Employees, whose mission is to transform your business into a Turbocharged Company second to none! If there is ever a time when the business needs all oars in the water pulling together, this has got to be it. Management cannot let past practices snuff out the creative initiatives employees can bring to this situation.

As Command and Control style management is ushered out, a new organizational structure takes its place. Managers, while still clearly responsible for the performance of the business, move into coaching and leadership roles. Employees are given substantially more latitude to "manage" themselves and now have input into operational and strategic planning, plus day-to-day decision making. The collective energy of teams, both formal and "ad hoc," become a vital part of the new organization.

Communicate What's Happening

Employees are usually very cynical about changes of this nature. They are going to have a hard time believing that, after years of "talking to a brick wall," management is suddenly ready to listen to them. If they have lived under a Command and Control management structure for many years, their doubts will be quite justified. And management's saying, "This time it will be different," will most certainly fall on skeptical, if not deaf, ears, until management's actions match its words.

This is usually not the first speech employees of underperforming companies have heard about changes designed to save the company. Most of these initiatives fizzled before they had a chance to start, indeed even before the employees left the meeting. Those that did survive the first 24 hours were generally rendered harmless by the third or fourth week and had little, if any, long-term effect. In such circumstances disdain for the management group would have only increased as employees watched, and often unwillingly took part in, such management "cures."

Thus, the challenge, once Command and Control management has been eliminated, is to convince employees that this time, things are truly different. Communication of this step is vital and key to the success of the remainder of the implementation plan. Management should start by acknowledging that it does not have all the answers. If it did, the company would not be where it is today. This will probably not be any significant news to the employees, who have long known this. What will be significant is the fact that they are hearing management admit it! The company needs the help of employees to solve its problems. That's news!

Next comes a very important face-to-face meeting between the CEO and *all* employees. Depending on the size of your company, this can be achieved in one group meeting, or a series of meetings. All meetings should be held in as concise a time frame as possible to get this initial announcement out and the transformation process started. Whenever possible, the meetings should be held on the employees' own "turf." This underscores the new philosophy that is being unveiled in this new organization— management is no longer more important than hourly workers.

None of the employees should be left out of these meetings. Second- and third-shift employees should not be asked to come in early, or stay late, for the convenience of management. Instead, if it is at all possible, the CEO should meet these employees on their own turf and during their regular shift. It is this type of action, no matter how inconvenient, that signals the end of Command and Control management and "business as usual."

We acknowledge that, depending on the size of your organization and the physical location of its employees, a full face-to-face meeting between all parties may not be possible. In such instances, we suggest employing videotapes, satellite link-ups, conference calls or whatever medium can get the message out as quickly and effectively as possible. In this circumstance, while the printed word is good, we encourage the use of those mediums that "show and tell." Our belief is that the closer management can get to face-to-face direct communication with its fellow employees, the more promising the outcome of these meetings will be.

At these gatherings, the message must be powerful, yet not excessively complicated. It is important that the remarks be informative, easy to understand, but not patronizing. After all, these are the very people who are going to help save the organization and transform it into a Turbocharged Company. These are the people to whom the CEO is saying, "I cannot do it by myself, but together, we can lift this company out of its troubles and secure a future for us all."

To illustrate the type of message involved, the following is an excerpt from a similar CEO talk at one of our underperforming clients.

"Ladies and gentlemen, it is a pleasure to be here today and to share some exciting information with you. As you all, no doubt, know, our company has not been performing as well as we would have hoped, or as well as we needed to over the past few years. We have had almost no growth in revenue over the past three years, and have experienced significant increases in quality problems and in scrap. Additionally, our shareholders have made it quite clear that they are not happy with our bottom line. While our business has been in a steady decline, the fortunes of several of our competitors have shown marked improvement both in total sales and market share. Each has come at our expense.

You are also painfully aware that we have tried many different avenues to improve this situation. Unfortunately, few of them have worked very well. I am sure you remember the consultant we brought in last year to help us address our quality problems. While we experienced some short-term improvements, the very same quality problems have resurfaced again—as bad as or worse than before. We attempted to improve our profits by a widescale layoff earlier this year. That approach proved even less successful, as with fewer people, our rate of on-time deliveries dropped significantly, resulting in many unhappy customers.

When I sat back and analyzed our experiences, it was apparent to me that management has not done a good job guiding this company to success. It certainly has not been for lack of trying—we have attempted many routes to improve things—it is just that none have been particularly effective. When I thought about it further, I wondered if our lack of effectiveness had anything to do with the way we were going about trying to solve the problem. I believe that there is a very strong likelihood that this is indeed the case.

I concluded that the task of achieving a healthy company in today's economic climate is pretty daunting—one that will require the best resources available to the company. It is in this area that I now realize we have been remiss. In the past, whenever we looked for solutions to our problems, we have always turned to senior management or outside consultants. This was "conventional wisdom." I have now concluded that we left a key source of talent and expertise out of this process—you! You are the people who work with our products every day, who have constant contact with our customers and understand their needs far better than senior management does. And I have no doubt that you have a wealth of knowledge about how to make things better around here.

Well, we may have missed golden opportunities in the past, but we are certainly not going to miss any more. Beginning today, our approach to running this company is going to be different. Gone are the days when you were told to do things by managers, with little or no understanding into the thinking behind what you were being told, or without any input from you as to how the problem or situation could be corrected. From now on, you will have the opportunity to participate in planning and decision-making processes. We want your involvement, your participation and your help.

In order to make the best possible suggestions, it is important that you be well informed. So, beginning today, you will have significantly expanded access to our performance information, so that everyone is aware of how the organization is doing against its goals and objectives.

At this stage, you are probably somewhat skeptical about all this. And really, I can't blame you. Having lived under our old management style for so long, why should you believe that things are going to change? I don't expect to convince any of you of this today. I believe it is our responsibility to communicate this to you with our actions as well as our words. I only ask one thing of you today—that you commit to keeping an open mind and let us prove the sincerity of our words to you. Don't let the memories of the past cloud the good that, working together, we can accomplish here.

Over the next few weeks, we will have several meetings with you to share more of the concepts involved with this process, and the role each of you will play. What I can tell you is that a large part of this process is centered on allowing you, the lifeblood of this organization, to play a significant role in making this a great company once again. It will be done with a combination of individual and team effort. Unlike anything you have done before, most of this work will be done in self-managed teams rather than traditional departments with traditional management hierarchy.

We are going to kick off this process with the creation of our first team—the Turbo Team. We have selected this name because this team will have the responsibility of overseeing the implementation of the Turbocharged Company Process. This is the key or lead team in this Process. I now invite you to help select the members of the Turbo Team. The team will be composed of 10 of the most capable people in the company, who possess the vision, energy and commitment to help this company succeed. The selections will be made from nominations from all the employees of the company. Please take the piece of paper being handed out and list up to 10 people you would like to see on this team. There are no pre-conditions or rules, except that you can only nominate up to four managers.

I'll be happy to answer any questions you may have at this point. When we are finished, please place your nominating forms in the box at the back of the room, either as you leave, or sometime before this shift is over. Thank you for your attention, and I look forward to working with all of you to turn our ailing business into a Turbocharged Company."

At this point, there is no turning back. The company has gone out on a limb by announcing the changes. Now it is time to deliver. Employees will be watching for those tell-tale signs that this speech is just like all the rest. It is only management's actions that will prove the sincerity of its commitment.

Please note that while we will refer to the first and main team as the Turbo Team, the name itself is not all that important. Other clients have used names like Restructuring Team, Vision Team and Focus Team as the name of this team. For clarity in our discussions, however, we will refer to this team as the Turbo Team.

We suggest 10 as the optimum number of team members. That is based on a company size of between 100 and 500 employees. If your organization is smaller, you will want to scale back the number of team members; however, we recommend an absolute minimum of four members to accomplish all that must be done. If your company is larger, you may wish to have more than 10 Turbo Team members. However, we would recommend a maximum size of 15, regardless of your company size. Any group larger than this becomes too unwieldy to perform the many duties assigned to this team.

Establishment of Turbo Team and Sub-teams

The nominations for the Turbo Team should be reviewed, and its members selected as quickly as possible. While we strongly encourage the use of employee nominations, we must state that these nominations should be used as a guide, not a rigid, cast-in-stone mandate. We suggest that the CEO, using the nominations as a tool, conduct informal interviews—chats—with each employee to determine firsthand if he or she would work out on the Team and what he "brings to the table." This helps ensure a good, well-rounded team. Management, using the nominations as an important guide, should ensure that the team is well represented with people of varying skills, experience levels, genders, races and functional areas within the organization.

If, due to the size of the organization or its locations or culture, the use of a nominating procedure will not work, management may appoint members to the Turbo Team. While we believe the nominating approach ensures early employee buy-in to the Turbocharged Company Process, it is not absolutely essential in making this process work.

The initial meeting of the Turbo Team will be a very interesting experience because it represents 10 or more people from various areas and levels within the organization coming together to work in a way that is, most likely, quite foreign to them. As previously noted, "managers" will only have a maximum of 40 percent of the team make-up, so they will not have the controlling vote— definitely a new experience for them.

It is our belief that the CEO should not be the Turbo Team leader. The CEO's function is to be the person to whom the team "sells" its ideas. The CEO should remain objective and, while being supportive of the work of the team, should ask a lot of tough questions, acting as the "devil's advocate." The team leader should initially be a team- and people-oriented Vice President or other senior manager who has good leadership and coaching skills. If such a person is not available, consider using an outside facilitator who is experienced in these areas.

The initial meeting of the Turbo Team should be held in a relaxed setting that ensures no interruptions. If this cannot be achieved at the company's facilities, consider having the meeting at a nearby hotel meeting room.

The Turbo Team leader should start the first meeting by establishing the following ground rules:

* All members of the team have equal standing, regardless of position in the company.

* No member will ever ridicule another member's ideas or suggestions, no matter how farfetched or inappropriate they may seem. (This is important because if people don't feel it is safe to express creative ideas, they will only present ideas without risk. Often the biggest advancements come from ideas that had initially seemed "off-the-wall.")

* Personal attacks between members are off-limits.

* Everything discussed in team meetings is confidential and not to be shared with other employees or anyone else until the team decides the time and format to share this information with others.

* While decisions should be made wherever possible by unanimous consent, if such agreement cannot be achieved, majority vote will rule.

At the first meeting, the CEO should be invited to devote about an hour outlining the Four Foundations of a Turbocharged Company and the company's commitment to attaining them. At this point, the CEO should wish the team the best of luck, express again his support for its work, and leave the team to get on with its task.

The Turbo Team functions as a central clearinghouse for ideas, the coordinator of activities and the group that keeps tabs on the Turbocharged Company Process. The sub-teams are the "worker teams" of this process. They are the ones who go out and spot problems, determine solutions and implement them.

Initially, there should be four sub-teams (one for each foundation):

A People Team—Responsible for ensuring the company Unleashes People Power.

A Customer Team—Responsible for ensuring the company Reveres its Customers and places customer satisfaction as its highest priority.

A Productivity Team—Responsible for ensuring the company never stops finding ways to improve productivity and lower operating costs.

A Market Team—Responsible for understanding the markets in which the company operates, the strengths and weaknesses of the company and its competitors, and for ensuring the company Dominates its MicroNiche(s).

Each sub-team should be composed of approximately six to ten members, at least two of whom should come from the Turbo Team. No more than 40 percent of each sub-team should be managers. Sub-team members should also be chosen based on the nominations for Turbo Team members. Again, try to get a fairly good representation of the company in each sub-team. Once sub-teams are selected, they must meet and choose a team leader, if one has not already been appointed by the Turbo Team.

Additional sub-teams should be created by the Turbo Team as the need arises. In every business setting, unique issues will arise that need to be analyzed, researched and improved. Sub-teams should be directed to deal with these issues. As an example, if the company is experiencing a cash crisis, it may be advisable to form a Cash Team, charged with searching for every possible way to generate cash.

It is important to note here that these teams do not replace the management structure. The purpose of these teams is to increase grass-roots employee involvement significantly and to identify new ideas for the business. Management still retains responsibility for the overall business. Yet the teams become an invaluable source of energy and creativity for management. As managers become more comfortable with their coaching and leadership role, they will give the teams more and more latitude to generate new ideas, and they will encourage the teams to implement those ideas. Management, which typically functions in somewhat of a vertical fashion, and teams, which generally function in a horizontal fashion, will then begin to overlay one another, interacting in a symbiotic, inter-dependent and mutually supportive fashion.

The work of the Turbo Team in the first weeks and months will be:

* **Identifying the major issues that will promote or hinder achieving Turbocharged Company status.** What are the major roadblocks or the major advantages in your company, and how can you get around one and take advantage of the other?

* **Developing a theme for the Turbocharged Company Process.** The theme will become the vehicle that galvanizes the employees into the Turbocharged Company Process. It gives them "something to hang their hats on."

* **Monitoring the direction and progress of the sub-teams.** Basically, keeping everyone "on-track."

* **Developing a realistic action plan and timetable.** Timetables for development of the action plan as well as the initial work of each sub-team must be developed, agreed upon and published.

* **Identifying resources that will be needed.** This can be financial, manpower, space, technical or other resources that will help each of the sub-teams or the Turbo Team do its job better and easier.

245

* **Presenting the action plan** to the CEO, Board of Directors and fellow employees—plus, if necessary, shareholders, lenders, creditors and any other interested parties. After all, the employees developed the plan and will play a significant role in implementing it; why shouldn't the Board see their earnest desire and sincerity?

* **Monitoring and coordinating the implementation of the action plan.** This is a very critical area for the Team, as it ensures all that was promised is delivered. As with most plans, implementation is key!

* **Ensuring the company never slides into complacency,** but instead continuously improves in each level of the Turbocharged Company Process.

The Turbo Team will probably need to meet almost daily at first, in order to get the process rolling. The first few meetings will probably be quite lengthy—they could last three to four hours. Some companies schedule a few one- or two-day retreats at the beginning of the process to foster this effort. Obviously while this is occurring, productivity could suffer somewhat. This is a short-term setback to ensure a long-term remedy to your company's ills. Later, as the process continues, the team can begin to cut back on its meetings, to two or three times each week. When the implementation process is well under way, meeting frequency can even be reduced to every two weeks or monthly.

The Turbo Theme

One of the first responsibilities of the Turbo Team is the development of the Turbo Theme. Far more than a catchy slogan or material for posters, the Turbo Theme provides a focal point for the new direction of the company. The theme signals what is important in the company.

While the concept of a theme sounds easy, its inception will only be the result of a lot of brainstorming. Once a theme has been developed, the Turbo Team should review it with all employees, to make sure everyone agrees the theme fits the situation and objectives of the organization.

The SIFCO team members concluded there were two primary reasons their company was not performing up to expectations. They were 1.) the lack of focus within the organization and 2.) the lack of total dedication to customer satisfaction. After brainstorming to come up with a Turbo Theme, this client emerged with:

For

Our

Customers'

Ultimate

Satisfaction

*It is interesting to note that several weeks after the SIFCO Turbo Theme was introduced, an hourly member of the Turbo Team was looking at the words printed above and noticed that the SIFCO name was contained within the word Sat**Is**Fa**C**ti**O**n. As word of this discovery spread around the company, employees suddenly understood the unique link between the Turbo Theme, customer satisfaction and their company.*

Another client learned, through its brainstorming process, that its problems could be attributed to 1.) an excessively complex process, 2.) a lack of attention to detail and follow-through and 3.) lack of focus on profitable business opportunities. Armed with this information, the Turbo team developed the following theme:

247

Simplify

Thorough

Profitable

— A well-oiled machine!

*In this company, the theme truly became a corporate mantra. If someone came up with an idea, a colleague could often be heard to say, "Have you **STP**[i]'d that idea?"*

Chrysler developed a "quasi-theme" around their renewal effort—"We're not the company we used to be, and we're not yet the company we're going to be." This message says a lot in just a few words. It says Chrysler is a very different company from the one that was teetering on bankruptcy once again in 1990. And while the company is certainly better-off for the progress it has made, it is far from satisfied. They still have a lot of work to do, and they're going to do a lot better. It is quite uplifting!

Spread the Word

It is vital that the work of the Turbo team, the sub-teams and the company's current situation be communicated to every employee. In this situation, you cannot over-communicate. Too little information can stall the Turbocharged Company effort—too much can never hurt.

The Turbo Team and each sub-team should publish a newsletter as soon as possible after the group has met. It is important that all the rest of the employees know what is going on—both to relieve their own anxiety and to stop the spread of

---

[i] STP is a registered trademark of the STP Oil and Refinery Company. The similarity between the theme and STP's trademark was totally unplanned and purely coincidental.

any rumors that can undermine the Turbocharged Company efforts. Each newsletter should address the following:

* The mandate, goals and objectives of the team

* The members of the team

* Issues that were discussed at the last meeting

* Problems faced, progress made and successes achieved

* Ways in which fellow employees can help the team

Every team should appoint two of its members to be its communications representatives. Their responsibility is publishing the team's newsletter. These people should take notes during the meetings of all subjects that could potentially be reviewed in the newsletter. The team should then decide, at the end of each meeting, what information can be released. It is not that the team is keeping secrets—it is just that some ideas, concepts and strategies are sometimes not ready to be shared. They may be premature, incomplete, dependent on other events or potentially threatening to some employees. The team needs to exercise due care in the release of information to the employee group.

Turbo Team members should conduct periodic (at least monthly) "Town Hall" meetings with their constituent group. Each employee should be assigned to a constituent group, depending on work function, location, shift or whatever criteria make sense. At these meetings, the Turbo Team member should review:

* The Four Foundations of a Turbocharged Company

* The mandates and goals of the Turbo Team and sub-teams

* The Turbo Theme

* Progress made, successes achieved or problems experienced by each team

* Suggestions from the employees

* Questions, comments and concerns

Although the Town Hall meetings and newsletters may seem a bit repetitious, they allow the employees to recall the information, fit all the pieces together and engage in discussion about the progress or concerns facing them. The Town Hall meeting helps the education process, as the information, first seen, is now heard. Where conducting "on-site" meetings is not feasible, due to multiple locations or the size of the group, alternative technologies should be considered. Chrysler, for example, uses its own satellite TV network to broadcast news of what is happening—at Chrysler plants and throughout the auto industry—to all of its plants 24 hours a day.

Additionally, it is vitally important that, as soon as practical, customers are informed as to what is happening at the company. Well-informed customers can be an asset, watching and helping your company in its turnaround efforts. Customers, hearing only pieces and parts of the process might assume, for example, that a palace revolt is taking place and that it would be better to steer business away from your firm. This would, obviously, be disastrous. Customers do not necessarily need to know all the "nitty-gritty," but they do need to know generally what is going on and how this will affect them. This is a great time to announce the refocusing of efforts of the organization toward customer satisfaction!

Finally, in the communication arena, there is the all-important Flash Report. We described this report in detail in Foundation Three. It is important that a newsletter and part of a Town Hall meeting be devoted to explaining the purpose and use of the Flash Report. You will be absolutely amazed at the business savvy the employees will develop, and how this translates to action, once they have this kind of information.

Put the "Pedal to the Metal"

At this point, you have laid the groundwork to facilitate the success of the Turbocharged Company Process in your own business. The teams have been Unleashed and are doing their work. Every aspect of the business is being analyzed and questioned. Employees have been provided with all the vital information about the company and have been given the knowledge of how to understand and use that information. Teams are working together to share information, discoveries and resolve problems.

The process gains momentum everyday. Crazy ideas and "If we could only . . ." dreams become the starting points for fantastic, implementable plans that lead to positive gains and efficiencies. "Heroes" will arise where you never thought they would—and surprise you with their tenacity and dedication to the company. "Crusaders" from all areas of the company will learn new skills and plunge into "foreign" areas as they work to develop and implement the action plan.

While the Turbocharged Company Process is evolving, the company continues to operate essentially as it did before the Process began. Significant change will not occur until all the sub-teams have completed their work and made their recommendations. Some changes, which do not require the full plan development, can and should be made at various times during the Process. There is no need to delay the elimination of the executive parking lot, for example. At the end of the process, the teams will present their plans to the CEO, the Board of Directors and their fellow employees. Once the plan is approved, the major changes will begin.

This initial Process of developing the preliminary action plan could take six to twelve weeks. Our experience has shown that if the Process lasts much longer, it will begin to drag. If the Process is shorter, sufficient time will not have been devoted to developing an effective plan.

Once approved, employees will take ownership of their plan. They will make the changes necessary, implement the new processes and behave like the company was their own—which by now it is!

During the implementation phase and thereafter, the Turbo Team should remain in place. Its function is to assist management in guiding the implementation of the plan, while ensuring the company remains committed to the Four Foundations. Sub-teams should also remain in place on an as-needed basis—while new sub-teams may be created to deal with fresh issues and challenges.

By focusing on the Four Foundations of a Turbocharged Company, management, the teams and all employees will have a roadmap to follow. The Process will soon show signs of Unleashing People Power. Employees will begin to feel the impact of the new culture, and they will become more and more comfortable with their roles in the pursuit of a better company. Their motivation, satisfaction and commitment to the company will soar.

As soon as People Power begins to be Unleashed, the stage will be set to change the way the company looks at its customers. Along with that, the company will begin the systematic search for lower costs, better methods and improved productivity. The people of your company, now invigorated and focused through their individual and team efforts, will drive the Process. Management, and other observers, will watch in amazement as they witness these new Corporate Crusaders pursue the company's crusade with a drive and determination previously unimagined.

These Unleashed People, as they Revere their Customers and Relentlessly Pursue Productivity, will open the door for the company to Dominate its MicroNiche. It is truly an unbeatable combination—fired-up employees, totally focused on customer satisfaction, operating in a highly productive and low-cost environment, ready to go out and make their company the best, most innovative business in its chosen field!

The Intensive Strategy Summary

* Abandon Command and Control management

* Direct communication to all employees

* Establish and empower the Turbo Team and the sub-teams

* Develop the Turbo Theme

* Establish regular employee communication vehicles, *i.e.* newsletters, Town Hall meetings

* Begin the Turbocharged Company Process

* Turbo Team and sub-teams review and formulate recommendations

* Recommendations made to CEO, Board and fellow employees

* Approval and Implementation

* Continual monitoring and enhancement

Moderate Strategy—"We're Doing Okay, But Want To Do Better"

In contrast to the company described in the previous section, where the wolves were at the door, the company may be doing okay, but you are not satisfied with its performance. Obviously some things are working well, or the company would not be performing at its current level. Clearly, however, there is need for improvement. Sales may be slipping, and/or competitors may be eating away at your market share—and profitability. Customer complaints may be on the rise, or you may be experiencing employee defections. Perhaps the organization may be, or is just about to be, hitting a plateau—seemingly stuck where it is, despite every attempt to do otherwise. Yet clearly you are not losing money quarter after quarter. You are not facing bankruptcy, liquidation or foreclosure. Bankers and suppliers are not treating you significantly differently. You are not in a crisis mode—you just want your company to do much better. Under this scenario, we suggest the **Moderate Strategy**—one of careful examination and controlled change.

Setting the Stage

The CEO should meet with all employees as we outlined in the Intensive Strategy. He or she should announce the commitment to becoming a Turbocharged Company. The Four Foundations should be introduced, and the company's commitment to starting the process by Unleashing People Power should be explained.

The concepts of teams and teamwork should be reviewed. If Command and Control management still exists in the organization, plans for its elimination should also be discussed.

This implementation strategy should be approached with less self-criticism than we illustrated in the Intensive Strategy. After all, the company is still achieving acceptable results; it just wants or needs to do better. The same candor is needed, however, as well as the same "walking the talk."

The CEO should set the vision—and report where the company is now in relation to those goals. Prior attempts to move the company from its present position, or improve results, should be noted, and the results frankly discussed. A clear message should be sent to all employees that the business is committed to becoming a Turbocharged Company. The company's goal is to surge ahead of its competitors, and achieving that will require doing things very differently.

Teams

The establishment and operation of the Turbo Team should proceed as we outlined in the Intensive Strategy. Again, while nominating team members is still the approach we advocate, many larger Turbocharged Companies name members to teams, and the approach has proven effective. This team should be charged with determining how to transform your organization into a Turbocharged Company. Its primary focus should be the achievement of the Four Foundations. The Turbo Team should start their work by performing a corporate self-evaluation of the company's present status relative to the Four Foundations: Are we effectively Unleashing People Power? Do we Revere our Customers? Are we structured to Relentlessly Pursue Productivity? And do we Dominate our MicroNiche(s)? The answers to these questions will provide the team with a roadmap of the areas on which to focus. If determined necessary by the Turbo Team, sub-teams can be formed on an as-needed basis, to deal with specific issues, processes or events.

While you want to communicate clearly that the organization is going to change significantly, it is important that everyone understands this will be done in an evolutionary, rather than revolutionary, manner. Utilizing this "evolutionary approach" is less disruptive to the ongoing business, your vendors, creditors, shareholders and customers. The key message is that employees, through team as well as individual efforts, will have a significant influence over the direction and success of the organization.

Theme

As described in the Intensive Strategy, one of the first tasks for the Turbo Team will be to establish a theme. The importance of a Turbocharged Theme cannot be emphasized enough—particularly in this situation where a crisis cannot serve as a rallying point, as it usually does in the Intensive Strategy. Again, it should reflect the individual situation of the organization, and its intended solution. We strongly encourage one continual theme, versus quarterly or yearly themes. Changing themes sends a signal to the organization that, perhaps, other things may have changed. The enterprise does not need these types of distractions.

Often, we find companies will evolve their Turbo Theme into their corporate mission statement. This expression of what a company stands for, and aspires to, is thus just an amplification of the ideals and concepts behind the original Turbo Theme.

Communication

Communication may be more critical in this implementation scenario than it is in the Intensive Strategy. In a crisis, everyone is eager to know what is going on and to embrace new ideas quickly. When things are going reasonably well, it is much more difficult to keep the energy level of the organization in a heightened state. The day-to-day details of the business can cloud the progress being made.

As in the Intensive Strategy, Town Hall meetings, newsletters and Flash Reports are essential parts of effective communication.

In addition, communications should also be extended to customers and vendors, to keep them apprised of the company's commitment to this Process.

Promoting the Process

Finally, as Unleashing People Power moves into high gear, it will be advisable to let this information become public. After all, you want bright people, looking for careers at progressive companies that treat their employees right, to be looking at your firm instead of your competitors. It will not only help hiring efforts, it will reinforce to employees that this is indeed real and that it will continue. As crazy as this may seem, the "power of print" cannot be underestimated. Tell the world how much productivity has increased, how quality has been improved, even how much Gainsharing dollars have been paid out! That kind of information is positive reinforcement of the hard work taking place on a daily basis at your company. It makes everyone— customers, vendors, stockholders and potential employees—sit up and take notice.

Energize

You have now set the stage for change in your organization. The suffocating aspects of Command and Control management have been abolished and replaced with the freshness and vitality of teams. You have identified areas that are problems, or perhaps just opened up all areas of the company for examination. You and your fellow employees want more out of your organization.

Now is the time to authorize the teams to go to work, and for management to step back and let them do it. Management must put aside its fears of losing control over the company, for they still have veto authority. They have to put aside their fears of "really screwing things up," because by Unleashing People Power, they have given employees the motivation, information and incentive not to let this happen.

Peter Lewis, CEO of Progressive Corporation, remarked that his only regret in the Turbocharged Company Process is that he did not start sooner. Our advice to you is that you should not look back or regret, but move forward with your fellow employees and colleagues, to realize the potential of your company.

The Moderate Strategy Summary

* Open communication with all employees to set vision and review process

* Establishment and empowerment of Turbo Team and other teams as required

* Development of the Turbo Theme

* Establishment of communication vehicles, *i.e.* Town Hall meetings, newsletters, Flash Report

* Research and analysis by teams—and development of recommendations

* Presentation of recommendations

* Implementation of recommendations and monitoring

* Communication to customers, vendors and the general public

Gradual Strategy—"We're Doing Great Now, But We Can Be Doing So Much Better"

This implementation strategy was designed for companies that are in no trouble at the present time. Sales and profits are right where they should be. People within the organization seem pleased with the progress the company has made. Everything seems to be going just fine.

Yet there may be a feeling that the company could be so much more than it is. Perhaps, instead of just being a big regional player, the thought of becoming the dominant national player no longer seems out of reach. Maybe the thought of serving the needs of your customer in a whole new way seems eminently logical after reading about Dominating your MicroNiche in this volume. Perhaps you suspect that there are areas where productivity could be improved. Or, the company may just need to work at improving a single area to make it even better. Whatever the situation, the company is ready to be positioned for change.

The implementation strategy outlined here reflects the need to take advantage of and build on, the company's current strengths—and yet instill the impetus for change that will take the company to even greater heights. While in some ways it may seem easier than the first two strategies, in many ways it is much more difficult. It is a lot harder to convince people that change is necessary when things are going well. For this reason, we recommend a paced approach that we call the **Gradual Strategy**.

Outlining the Vision

The CEO should meet with all employees, as we outlined in the first two implementation strategies. This talk is key to the Process, as it will outline for all employees just what the vision is—where the company will be headed, why it should be headed that way, and how this future vision builds on today's reality.

The talk should start with a review of the company's present position—its strengths and potential weaknesses. The reasons for its present success should also be reviewed. Then the CEO should broadly outline where the company could be—where its potential is and how it can get there. The vision will not be a complete package, all tied up with implementation steps and strategies, for that work will come later. Yet it should be something all employees can visualize and relate to. Chrysler's current mission, "To be the premier North American car and truck company by 1996, and worldwide by 2000" is an example of such a vision. There are no details, no "How are we going to do that," yet it is something everyone can embrace.

Key to the success of this address, and indeed the entire effort, is the need to keep much of the organization focused on today's business, while teams spend time planning for the future. Obviously if everyone is focused on the future and no one is concentrating on today's customer, the base business will begin to suffer.

The Turbo Team

At the conclusion of this message, the CEO should name a cross-functional team to spearhead the effort to "flesh out" the CEO's vision and outline the changes that must take place. This team, like the Turbo Teams discussed in the first two strategies, should be composed of people within the organization with a breadth of knowledge about the company, its customers and its way of doing business. While it may seem natural to fill this group with senior management, our experience has shown that taking people from all levels within the organization will significantly enhance the value this team can offer. Senior managers, while perhaps seeing the vision a little clearer, are less knowledgeable about operational issues that can greatly affect the success of this transition. Similarly, operational people, who may get bogged down in the details, will need someone to continually hold the vision for the team to see, and focus on. Additionally, a team with representation from all levels fosters broader employee buy-in and commitment—hence contributing to Unleashing People Power.

In contrast to our two previous strategies where announcement of the Turbocharged Company Process, Four Foundations, Turbo Teams and the Turbo Theme were part of the initial employee communication, in this approach we start with the desired result.

The vision has been outlined and understood by the team. "Now how do we get there from here?" is the question that must be posed to the team. "How do we take our present strengths, competitive advantages and market position and leverage them to expanding the business? How can we find out what else our customers need, and how we can supply this product or service? Are there other customers whom we could serve that would be a natural adjunct to our present business?"

As the team seeks answers to these questions, it will utilize the Four Foundations as a guide. The company can only leverage its present position if it understands MicroNiche strategy. It can only seek to expand its support of present customers and future ones by enhancing its Reverence for those Customers. New products or services will only be marketable if they are produced as cost-effectively as possible, hence Relentlessly Pursuing Productivity. And all this will require Unleashing People Power in order to be accomplished.

By working in this manner, the Turbocharged Company Process becomes less of a revolutionary approach and more the answer to, "How do we get there from here?"

Implementing the Process

The Turbo Team, as it reviews its work, might form sub-teams to deal with specific issues. To work on the question of leveraging the company's present strengths, for example, a Market Team may be formed, focusing on MicroNiche techniques. To determine the needs of present and future customers, a Customer Team may be formed. Further, most companies would certainly want to establish a People Team to ensure People Power is Unleashed throughout the organization. And on it goes.

The sub-teams should be composed from the appropriate functional areas of the company. The teams should be empowered to search for solutions to problems, or ways to enhance opportunities, yet they should not be empowered to implement such plans. Under this implementation strategy, change must be carefully orchestrated to ensure minimal disruption within the organization. The changes to be made here will evolve gradually, systematically. It is vital that all recommendations be prudently considered, and their implementation carefully planned.

Theme

Just as in the first two strategies, a theme is vitally important to the success of this project. It becomes the umbrella under which all efforts are developed and reviewed. It lends consistency to a seemingly disparate group of teams as they work to outline the steps necessary to achieve the vision set before them. It should reflect the organization and its very distinct needs.

Communication

Clear and constant communication, always an important part of any implementation strategy, is vital to the success of this one. Such communication must:

> * Keep the vision in front of all employees, so it does not become lost in the day-to-day shuffle.

> * Keep the work of the teams publicized as a reminder of the vision and the new era the company is entering. This also acknowledges the work each team is doing, providing team members further encouragement.

> * Keep the employees focused on serving today's customer to the very best of their ability, even as the organization moves into other areas or moves to expand its product/service offerings.

> * As appropriate, "flesh out" the vision described to employees to bring the organization "up to speed" gradually before changes are made.

This communication can take the form of Town Hall meetings, Flash Reports, newsletters, video conferences, special "to the employee's home" mailings—whatever vehicle, or combination thereof, can best get your message across.

Further, once the process is well underway, communication to customers, vendors, shareholders and the general public is in order. Every group has separate needs and concerns, all of which must be addressed. Every group will also have to be "brought up to speed" with where the company is headed and how they fit in. Customers will want assurance that they will not be deserted or harmed as the company goes off and enters another MicroNiche. Vendors will want to know their role, while shareholders will want to know what this will mean for them—both long- and short-term. Finally, the general public will be interested in how you are continuing your success and building for an even brighter future. Such exposure helps not only recruiting efforts, but vendor selection, shareholder relations and potential customer recruiting.

"Make it Happen"

The challenge in a business that is currently successful is breaking out of the complacency of doing exactly what you are doing today. Turbocharged Companies realize this and stay hungry for new opportunities to serve their customers, grow their MicroNiche(s) and enhance productivity. That sense of dedication, that fervor, must be brought to the successful organization to ensure it continues to move ahead. The CEO must constantly be challenging the organization to reach new heights. To bravely go where the corporation did not think it could go—and do it successfully.

The Gradual Strategy has the advantage of sufficient time to test and try all changes before full implementation. There is time to coordinate all the steps to move the organization consistently toward the future organization. The end result will be the same— a Turbocharged Company—only the route getting there will be different.

Gradual Strategy Summary

* Outline the vision—where the company is and where it could be

* Establish the Turbo Team

* Establish sub-teams as necessary

* Develop a theme

* Implement the Process in a carefully orchestrated fashion

* Communicate—to employees, vendors, customers, shareholders and the public

* Make it happen

What Can I Do?

Everyone who reads this book will be in a slightly different situation. This will primarily be due to the present state of the company you run or work for. Clearly the role of all employees in a company that is in a serious financial crisis will be more urgent and intensive than, for example, the role of employees in a company that is basically healthy, but still wants to improve.

Another distinction might be the size of your organization. You may work for a division of a large conglomerate with thousands of employees or you may work in a smaller company with 20 or 30 employees.

A third distinction will be your position within the overall organization. Obviously the role a CEO would have in transforming an organization—any size organization—into a Turbocharged Company will be substantially different from the role of a department, branch, plant or division manager. In addition, the role of non-management employees will also be different from the CEO or other managers' roles. And that's the point of this chapter—what role should you play?

To be sure, becoming a Turbocharged Company involves change, and many people are not comfortable with change. The key to success in this Process is to know more about what will be expected of you during and after this Process, as well as the skills and attitudes you will need to utilize or employ that perhaps you currently do not have, or use on a very frequent basis.

THE DYNAMICS OF ROLES AND SKILLS IN A TURBOCHARGED COMPANY
(Figure 4)

Position	Role in a traditional company	Role in a Turbocharged Company	Skills/Attitudes Needed for New Role
Board Member	Oversight Sounding board Devil's advocate	Cheerleader Oversight Sounding board Devil's advocate	Challenge status quo Eager to change Confidence in People Power Positive attitude
Chief Executive Officer	"Buck Stops Here" Primary Decision Maker Sets Vision and Mission "Do as I say, not as I do" mentality	Guides interactive process to establish vision Coaches individuals/teams to make decisions Role model for employees	Flexible Seek other views Active listener Communication skills Delegate decision making
Corporate Officer, Senior Manager	Supervises execution of strategies/plans Holds employees' feet to the fire	Team leader or member Coach and facilitator May continue to have line responsibilities	Flexible Work with others throughout the organization as equals Coaching and motivating Active listener
Middle Manager Department Head, Supervisor, Foreman	Communicates directives of senior management to line employees	Team leader or member Works to communicate with coworkers to identify and solve problems Resource for team Coach and facilitator	Works with others throughout the organizaton as equals Analytical problem solving Coaching and motivating Active listener
Non-management employee	Performs tasks assigned by managers	Team leader or member Participates in problem solving Helps fashion vision and goals Exercises initiative	Evolve from complaining about problems to solving them Analytical skills for use in identifying causes of problems Take responsibility for own actions Initiative

To assist you in this process, we developed this guide, and the accompanying chart on the left (figure 4), to serve as an aid to understanding your role.

The Turbocharged Company Process is one that can successfully be implemented in almost any organizational structure. Individual departments within an organization can become "Turbocharged Companies," and often the example they set spreads like wildfire throughout the organization. Soon the entire company will want to know more about becoming a Turbocharged Company. It may not happen overnight, but it will happen.

Individual **non-management employees** have a very important role in a Turbocharged Company environment. Your role moves from performing tasks to participating in teams, in problem solving and in planning. Armed with the knowledge of the details of your function, and the overall goals of the company, you are uniquely positioned to become a major asset to your company.

To do so will require keeping an open mind—being receptive to new ideas. It requires moving from complaining about problems to solving them. And your new role means that you take responsibility for your performance and that of the team in which you work.

As an individual **Department, or Branch Manager**, you may not be able to abolish Command and Control management throughout the organization, yet you can within your own group. You may not be able to abolish the executive parking lot and other perks, yet you could give up your own reserved spot. In so doing, you will be telegraphing the same powerful message to your employees—the only thing that has changed is the scale. You can begin treating your former subordinates as colleagues, and begin Revering Your Customers—those internal and external groups that rely on the product or service your group supplies. Your role in implementing the Turbocharged Company concepts can be more hands-on, due to the size of your operation.

Building on this, you can examine your own MicroNiche. Just what product or service are you providing—and who is your customer? After you have defined that, you can then follow up with an examination to determine what other products or services you can provide to your customers. Finally, you can explore how you can do the job better, faster, cheaper and with more value to the customer.

Your role moves from the transmitter of senior management's wishes to coach and counselor. You may be a team member, or a team leader—yet regardless of your position, the respect you earn comes from your contribution to the team, not via title or status.

As a **Plant or Division Manager**, your work group is usually pretty well self-contained. In some ways, your work to transform your organization is easier because of this. Yet it is also larger. For this reason, you cannot lead the charge all by yourself. Your role will be a combination of the CEO role as outlined in this book, along with the supportive executive. While you can foster the movement to become a Turbocharged Company, the real efforts must come from your employees. It is they who need to catch the vision of what your plant or division could become. This will fuel the changes necessary throughout your organization.

So how do you do this? We suggest distributing a few copies of this book to key individuals within your organization. The books can be delivered with an "I think there are some good ideas here. Read it over and let's talk about it." Your group of key individuals should come from all levels within your organization. Utilizing this approach, the preconceived notions of one group will not influence the outcome of the whole plant or division. Meet with your group, talk about the Turbocharged Company Process and what it could mean to the organization. Then begin taking the steps appropriate for your implementation strategy.

While you continue to have line responsibilities, your role in a Turbocharged Company environment changes to coach and facilitator. Your new role requires the ability to work with all levels within the organization, coaching and motivating each team to achieve its desired goals.

Finally, if you are the **CEO** of an organization, your role will be much the same as the Plant or Division Manager, with the exception that at this level of change within the organization, you will undoubtedly require Board approval. In this regard, your role also includes championing this process through Board approval. This doesn't mean you make the presentation to the Board, but you are the one "friendly face" and "guaranteed vote" in the room.

Your role becomes one of guiding the vision and helping the teams by acting as a sounding board. The "buck-stops-here" approach gives way to listening, being the devil's advocate, and encouraging the work of each team. Your ability to relinquish power is seen as a measure of your strength, not a sign of weakness.

If you are a **Board member**, your role expands to include being a cheerleader, as you celebrate the victories the Process can bring and spur the teams to further advances by always challenging the status quo. It is an exciting role.

While everyone's role in the Turbocharged Company Process will clearly be a little different, the basic thrust should be the same for all—a commitment to ignite the business to soar ahead of the competition, by Unleashing People Power, Revering Customers, Relentlessly Pursuing Productivity and Dominating MicroNiches.

The View in the Rear-View Mirror

There is no more rewarding experience than being involved with success—being on the winning team. The exhilaration that will run through your veins is the best stimulant money can buy. Success just seems to breed success, and suddenly all the hard work seems not only worthwhile—but fun! Southwest's Kathy Pettit put it this way:

> *"When my alarm goes off in the morning, I'm charged. When I go to bed at night, I'm looking forward to getting up. I want to come here. On days when my son is sick and I can't come in, I'm miserable. It is like having an invitation to a great party, and you can't go!"*

Fun aside, the worry in the pit of your stomach has been replaced by the joy in your heart as you survey your fellow employees and realize that together, you have changed the company for the better. You have made it a great place to work.

The competitors that you once feared have been passed by. The company has surpassed them, not as a deliberate goal, but as a result of serving your customers better. You and your fellow employees can hold your heads high, knowing you are now the Leader of the Pack. What a feeling!

Take a look at your organization. If you are consistently outperforming your competitors in terms of profits and sales, and generating superior returns for your stockholders, then you need take no further action. You undoubtedly are a Turbocharged Company; yet because of this, you are probably still looking for new ways to motivate employees, increase customer satisfaction and enhance your competitive advantages. We hope this book has given you plenty of ideas in these areas.

But if your company is not quite meeting these standards; if it could definitely make improvements in these areas; then we encourage you to implement the Turbocharged Company Process. By making this decision, you will make your organization a more stimulating place in which to work—with increased productivity, lower costs, and more profit. You will have happier customers, a more energetic organization and more control over your destiny than you ever thought possible. You will be glad you started the process—and you will not want to ever turn back.

Over the years, our consulting firm, The Parkland Group, has had the good fortune of working with a number of Turbocharged Companies. Some were clients, others were companies that generously participated in the research for this book. During the same time, we have also witnessed more than our share of businesses that were quite the opposite. The contrast between the two types of companies is absolutely staggering. The joy and energy of people associated with a Turbocharged Company is simply incredible. Seeing the two, you have to wonder why anyone would want to work in any organization that is not a Turbocharged Company.

We hope that you will unlock the secrets to success within your own organization—that you will be able to experience first hand the wonderful difference between the rat race of a "traditional" company and the fun and rewards associated with a Turbocharged Company. The key to unlocking your organization from the shackles of mediocrity is in your hands. We wish you our very best!

Let's Get Turbocharged![i]

---

[i] "Let's Get Turbocharged" is a trademark of The Parkland Group, Inc.

Appendix A

The following pages contain a brief synopsis of the main questions and answers many people have when first involved with teams. This guide is not all encompassing, yet quite useful. Further information is located in the text, and a wealth of information on teams can be found in the sourcebooks listed at the end of this section. While establishing teams is not the only ingredient necessary to create a Turbocharged Company, teams do play a critical role in the implementation of all Four Foundations, particularly Unleashing People Power.

With this in mind, here are the most common questions we receive about teams:

1. Where did the idea of teams originate?

The concept of working in teams has been around for a very long time. W. Edward Deming, the father of the Quality movement, was a major proponent of teams, and is often credited with vaulting Japanese manufacturing to a dominant position in the 1980s. Deming believed that every process could be continuously improved, and that the commitment and energy of people plays a significant role in process improvement.

2. Why are teams necessary? Why not just have strong managers?

The challenges of business today are just too complex for one person to be able to analyze all the data, consider the wide array of available options, and make decisions that are right for the organization. Teams permit this responsibility to be spread across a group of people who can devote their collective energies, knowledge and experience to the problem.

The manager, rather than being burdened with the pressure of having to be wiser than Solomon, can now function more as a coach to the team, giving them guidance and checking their logic and assumptions. In the end, decisions are made using the wisdom of the manager *and* the collective thought processes of the team.

3. How do teams affect employee commitment?

Employees who are able to participate in the search for new ideas and solutions to problems will feel far greater *ownership* in the ideas, and therefore be more committed to ensuring that their implementation is a success.

4. Are there different types of teams?

Yes, there are three primary types of teams; **project teams, process teams and functional teams.** Project teams, for example, are teams assembled to deal with one specific project. This might be moving to a new facility, or starting up a new product or service.

Process teams, on the other hand, are set up to work on a specific work process. This may be improving the scheduling in the press room of a stamping manufacturing company, or reviewing the credit approval process to determine if it can be streamlined. It is important to note that the objective of process teams is always to achieve substantial improvement over what is happening when the team first starts.

Functional teams are charged with performing the normal function of a business at a higher level than could be achieved by a traditional Command and Control departmental structure. Functional teams can run an office, a specific function or a group of functions in one area.

5. Who are the members of a team?

Any employee can be eligible to serve on a team. Many teams have people from various levels and departments within the company. The major criteria to be a successful team member are a positive attitude, an open mind and willingness to be flexible. Every team has a Team Leader, whose job is to plan the agendas of team meetings, keep the team on schedule and help the team work through problems.

6. What objectives should a team have?

Big ones, meaningful ones, ones that almost make the team members want to quit because the challenge is so great. This is when the greatest progress is made.

7. How does a team get started?

First, set a clear goal. Then, educate the team members about their responsibilities as team members, how they can get needed information and how to analyze such data. Then let them go.

8. What are the keys to team success?

a. Clear, challenging goals.

b. Respect for each member, their ideas and concerns.

c. An understanding that each member is equally responsible for the team's success, and accountable to all other teammates.

d. Use of in-depth objective analysis, supported by solid facts.

e. The continual, intensive search for "break-through" ideas.

9. How should the team accomplish its task?

A team should use four phases of analysis and action, namely:

    a. Collect meaningful, objective data relative to the process or problem utilizing:

* Pareto Charts	* Decision and Process Trees
* Control Charts	* Work Flow Diagrams
* Timelines	* Checklists to track activities, etc.

    b. Understand the root causes of the problem, instead of just the symptoms.

    c. Develop ideas, options and solutions based on reasonable analysis, utilizing the brainstorming process.

    d. Apply those solutions, utilizing a thorough, well-supported implementation plan.

10. How should a team make decisions?

Decisions should preferably be made by unanimous agreement. The team should exercise patience and consideration, by continuing to examine and discuss issues that are not yet unanimously agreed upon. Rather than viewing dissenters as impediments to progress, the team should have a positive attitude to differences of opinion, and view them as a chance to re-examine the status quo. Team members who have reservations about decisions should be asked to clearly state their concerns, and the team should analyze their proposed solutions in view of these concerns. If a minority of team members still have reservations, they should be asked if they *strongly disagree* with the decision. If, after debate, they do not strongly disagree, majority vote should rule. If any team member strongly disagrees, the team should "go back to the drawing board" and re-examine the issue until strong disagreements can be removed.

11. Once a team is started, how can it keep moving?

All team members should keep in mind the team's mandate—its goal to achieve. Set a deadline for an end result, be that a report, an action, or whatever. Then keep measuring the team's progress against that deadline and its original mandate.

12. How can we keep team meetings as productive as possible?

Always have an agenda with a time allocation for each item. Ensure that each member is prepared, and that their assignment is complete. Ensure meetings start promptly, cannot be missed and cannot be interrupted. Keep minutes of each meeting, and circulate them promptly.

Start every meeting by asking each team member to state in one to three minutes their feelings and concerns about the progress of the team to-date. End every meeting by asking every team member, using the same time restriction, how he/she felt about the meeting.

13. What are some other common team problems, and what can be done about them?

a. Lack of progress, floundering—Action: Review the team's goals, summarize its progress to date, list its obstacles, then tackle each one-by-one.

b. Overbearing or dominating members—Action: Focus on participation from all members, on the importance of objective analysis, not the unsubstantiated opinions of the loudest member(s).

c. Lack of broad participation—Action: Every member should be encouraged to participate. Discussions can be directed to less outspoken members to elicit their insights, and presentation can be required from more members on important issues. Fundamentally, those quieter members must understand how important it is to the team's success that they contribute their unique views and perspective.

14. How can a team be controlled?

The starting point is a clear definition of the team's goals—the team's mission must clearly be spelled out when the team is formed.

In addition, a technique that helps many teams is to have the support and advice of a Sponsor, or the counseling of a Team Expert. A Sponsor is a member of senior management who helps guide the team and acts as a liaison for the team with senior management. The Sponsor also helps the team locate resources that will be needed to implement their plans. A Team Expert is someone very knowledgeable about teams, who is available to advise the team on how to work best as a team. In larger companies, this might be a full-time employee. Other companies often utilize outside consultants.

15. How can conflict between members be resolved?

While differences in opinion are important to creative brainstorming, serious conflict is a major threat to team success. It can upset a team's chemistry and balance. When team members disagree, common sense dictates that they should resolve it privately, outside the team. The next best solution is for the Team Leader and or Team Sponsor to play a role of an intermediary—counseling the two people while helping them communicate with one another to resolve their conflict. If this approach fails, the entire team may have to become involved. In rare and last-resort instances, if the differences cannot be effectively resolved, the team may have to ask one or both members to leave the team, for the good of the team.

16. What if team members are not team players?

Great care should be exercised when setting up teams to ensure that team members are good team players. Despite this, there will always be a few people who do not function well in a team environment. If this happens, the Team Leader, the Sponsor or the Team Expert should try to counsel the member and help him/her acquire team skills. If this is unsuccessful, as a last resort the member may have to be asked to leave the team.

17. What are some ways to build team spirit?

a.)Team members can get to know one another better by going on a retreat together, or participating in an activity together, *i.e.,* going to a ball game.

b.)Team members can work in each other's jobs for a day.

c.)A team member can sit and observe the meeting of the Team as an independent bystander, then report to the team what he or she has learned.

d.)Team members can become closer by encouraging and practicing open, honest communication at all times.

18. Does a team eventually replace line management?

In some cases self-directed teams begin to manage themselves and eliminate the need for direct supervision. Often, in traditionally-run companies, the success of a project team is a great motivator to the employees. With management's approval, they form functional teams to more effectively operate the business. For example, the team members charged with improving the manufacturing process of one firm were encouraged by plant management to form teams to handle the scheduling, procurement and other functions the team had reviewed.

19. Does management give up control to teams?

No. Management always has the responsibility for the company. However, as managers become more comfortable with teams, they may delegate more and more responsibility to teams.

20. How are team leaders selected?

In some situations, the team leader is appointed by management, in other situations the team elects its own leader. The leader should be the most qualified person on the team, and does not necessarily have to be a manager. On some teams, the leader may be the person with the most expertise in the process being reviewed. On other teams, the leader may be the person most knowledgeable and skilled at leading a team.

21. Define the role of the Team Leader.

The team leader 1.) sets the pace of the team through its agenda and monitors its progress towards its goal(s); 2.) facilitates discussions and decisions by the group; 3.) guides the team in the event of lack of direction, progress or conflict. The leader is not the "boss" of the team and it is not his/her job to impose his/her will upon the team.

22. In a team environment, what role does management play?

The roles of coaches, cheerleaders, motivators, sounding boards, devil's advocates and resource providers are ascribed to management. Management needs to provide the teams with the opportunity to succeed through training, providing clear goals and the appropriate support.

23. Do teams have the authority to implement their actions without management's approval?

Whether they do or do not depends on the mandate they received from management at their inception. Management should always strive to give teams authority to implement their actions, without coming back to them for approval. However, in cases where team actions impact other areas of the business, its strategic direction or major policies, the team should be required to get management's approval. Management's review should be done expeditiously to avoid disrupting the momentum of the team.

24. How can I be a more effective team member?

    a.   Be on time to meetings and do the work requested of you.

    b.   Respect others

    c.   Listen actively to the ideas of other members.

    d.   Participate fully.

    e.   Constantly strive to improve yourself and learn.

25. Do teams ever end?

Yes, once they accomplish all their goals.

For Additional Information on Teams

Fisher, Kimball. *Leading Self-Directed Work Teams.* McGraw-Hill, Inc. 1993

Katzenbach, Jon R. and Smith, Douglas K. *The Wisdom of Teams.* Harvard Business School Press. 1993

Manz, Charles C. and Sims, Henry P. Jr. *Business Without Bosses.* John Wiley & Sons, Inc. 1993

Scholtes, Peter R. *The Team Handbook.* Joiner Associates Inc. 1988

Tjosvold, Dean. *Working Together to Get Things Done.* Lexington Books. 1986

We would be delighted to receive feedback or comments about this book and your company's experiences in striving to become a Turbocharged Company. Please contact us at:

The Parkland Group, Inc.
1375 East Ninth Street
Suite 1350
Cleveland, Ohio, USA 44114
216/ 621-1985 (phone)
216/621-1894 (facsimile)
Parkland1@aol.com (e-mail)

Notes

[1] Lawrence, Jennifer. A tale of 2 airlines: Up & down in Dallas. *Advertising Age.* May 30, 1994. p38

[2] Southwest Airlines Co. 1993 Annual Report

[3] Progressive Corporation 1994 Annual Report. Letter to the Shareholders

[4] The Home Depot 1994 Annual report

[5] "Home Depot's Shadow CEO," *Georgia Trend.* March 1993. p30

[6] "The 20% Club Is No Longer Exclusive," *The Wall Street Journal.* May 4, 1995. pC1

[7] "Home Depot's Shadow CEO," *Georgia Trend.* March 1993. p30

[8] "Quick Hits, Talking Business," *Performance.* November 1994. p11

[9] Quinn, Judy, "What a Work Out!" *Performance.* November 1994. p62

[10] Caminiti, Susan, "What Team Leaders Need To Know," *Fortune.* February 20, 1995. p93

[11] Chrysler Corporation 1993 Report to Shareholders. p5

[12] Loeb, Marshall, "Empowerment that Pays Off," *Fortune.* March 20, 1995. p145

[13] "Empowered Employees Earn Their Stripes," Book Review. *National Productivity Review.* Spring 1994. p303

[14] Quinn, Judy, "What a Work Out!" *Performance.* November 1994. p58

[15] Lutz, Robert, Speech to Northrup-Grumman Corp. Strategic Leadership Conference. April 10, 1995

[16] "Brief Cases," *Performance.* March 1995. p21

[17] "Marcus, Blank Keep Depot on Service track," *BSHC.* April 1995. p22

[18] Robert Half International, Inc. 1994 Salary Guide

[19] Loomis, Carol J., "Dinosaurs?" *Fortune.* May 3, 1993. p42

[20] Murray, Matt. "Amid Record Profits, Companies Continue to Lay Off Employees," *The Wall Street Journal.* May 4, 1995. p1

[21] "News & Notes," *Potentials in Marketing.* June 1995. p10

[22] Interview. June 26, 1995

[23] MBNA Corporation 1993 Annual report. p8

[24] Tichy, Noel M. and Sherman, Stratford, "Jack Welch's Lessons for Success: Control Your Destiny or Someone Else Will," book review, *Fortune.* January 25, 1993. p86

[25] The Home Depot Corporate Social Responsibility Report-1994. p1

[26] Chrysler Corporation 1993 Report to Shareholders. p15

[27] Fierman, Jaclyn, "The Death and Rebirth of the Salesman," *Fortune.* July 25, 1994. p80

[28] The Limited, Inc. 1990 Annual report. p14

[29] "Maintaining the Momentum," Chrysler Corporation. 1994

[30] Maietta, Vince, "Saturn Turns Lemon into Lemonade in Huge Recall," *The Business Journal/Serving Phoenix and the Valley of the Sun.* August 20, 1993. p39

[31] "Snacks, Balloons and a Recall," *Business Week.* August 23, 1993. p34

[32] Heil, Gary; Parker, Tom and Tate, Rick. *Leadership and the Customer Revolution.* p66

[33] The Limited, Inc. 1990 Annual report. p16

[34] Hewlett Packard 1994 Annual report. p9

[35] Eastman Chemical Company ad reprint. "If it were easy, anyone could do it."

[36] "Jack Welch's Lessons for Success," Book Excerpt, *Fortune.* January 23, 1993. p86

[37] Quinn, Judy, "What a Work Out!" *Performance.* November 1994. p58

[38] Jackson, Kathy, "Tutor and Pupil, Chrysler adopts Freudenberg-NOK as its lean-manufacturing mentor," *Automotive News.* December 19, 1994. p1

[39] Jackson, Kathy, "Chrysler execs help look for gains on O-Ring line," *Automotive News.* December 19, 1994. p1

[40] Chrysler Corporation 1994 Report to Shareholders. "To Our Shareholders" p3

[41] Chrysler Corporation 1993 Report to Shareholders. "To Our Shareholders." p8

[42] Chrysler Corporation 1994 Report to Shareholders. p12

[43] Chrysler Corporation 1993 Report to Shareholders. p13

[44] Overman, Stephanie. "No Frills HR at Nucor," *HR Magazine.* July 1994. p56

[45] Quinn, Judy, "What a Work Out!" "Best Practices Make Perfect," sidebar article, *Performance.* November 1994. p62

[46] Chrysler Corporation 1993 Report to Shareholders. "To Our Shareholders." p7

[47] Allied Signal 1994 Annual Report/10K. p6

48 "Quick Hits - Talking Business," *Performance*. November 1994 p11

49 Tully, Shawn. "Raiding a Company's Hidden Cash," *Fortune*. August 22, 1994. p82

50 Ibid.

51 Ibid.

52 DiCarlo, Lisa. "To Trim Inventory, Compaq Banking on Built-to-Order," *PC Week*. February 20, 1995. p107

53 "Management Brief, Crunch at Chrysler," *The Economist*. November 12, 1994. p93

54 Ibid.

55 Norton, Leslie P., "Crowded Fairways," *Barron's*. April 12, 1995. p27

56 Sabbath, Donald, "Company Profits from Tithing," *The Plain Dealer*. February 12, 1994. pC1

57 Weber, Joseph, "How To Rope 'Em With Plastic," *Business Week*. September 26, 1994. p135

58 Bounds, Wendy, "Kodak Under Fisher: Upheaval in Slow Motion," *The Wall Street Journal*. December 22, 1994. pB1

59 Kebler, Jack, "Quality Woes Anger Eaton," *Automotive News*. June 27, 1994. p1

60 Gross, Ken, "The Moving Target," *Automotive Industries*. March 1995. p108; Morrison, Mike. Chrysler Corporation

61 Deavenport, E. W. *Unlocking the Potential of the Human Mind and Spirit*. address to the South Carolina Hall of Fame. May 12, 1994.

62 Beirne, Mike, "Nucor shows its pricing based on simple 1+1=2," *American Metal Market*. May 11, 1994. p6

63 Bloomberg Business News, as reprinted in *The Plain Dealer*. November 1, 1994. p2C

64 Patterson, Gregory. Sears To Spin Off Allstate; Brennan To Retire In 1995. *The Wall Street Journal*. 11/11/94. pA1

65 Treece, James B., "Kmart: Slick Moves-Or Running in Place," Top of the News. *Business Week*. January 17, 1994. p28

66 Ibid.

67 Bird, Laura, "March Retail Sales . . ." *The Wall Street Journal*. April 7, 1995. pA1

Index

300

O

P

Q

Quality Control, 151
Quick Response
    GE's inventory system, 158
Quillen, Clyde
    Chrysler Corporation, 43

R

Relentlessly Pursue Productivity, 19,
    139, 180, 187, 189, 201, 263
    defined, 17
Restructuring Team. *See* Turbo Team
Return on Assets Managed, 167
    effect on ROE, 168
    working capital discussion, 169
Return on Shareholder Equity
    historical average, 11
Return on Shareholders' Equity
    defined, 11
    how ROAM can improve, 168
    Turbocharged Companies, 11
Revering Your Customers, 19, 139,
    201, 263
    defined, 17
    second Foundation, 18
ROAM. *See* Return on Assets
    Managed
ROE. *See* Return on Shareholders'
    Equity
Ronald McDonald House. *See*
    Southwest Airlines
Roos, Larry A.
    Nucor Corporation, 87, 210

S

Salesperson
    non customer revering, 102
Sam's Club, 220
Saturn Motors, 99
    customer service, 103
SCORE. *See* Chrysler Corporation
Scott Paper, 203
Scott, Bryant
    Home Depot, 74

Sears, Roebuck & Company
    drop from #1 spot, 218
SIFCO Forge Group, 7, 18, 32, 48,
    82, 151
    "rebirth"-evidence of, 7
    about, 6
    customer identification, 107
    daily Flash Report, 63
    employee involvement, 63
    employee self-esteem, 61
    employees, 7
    forge shop, 150
    gainsharing plan, 70
    initial situation, 6
    job rates, 77
    management evaluation, 62
    quoting process, 146
    results, 62
    Turbo Theme, 247
SIFCO Industries
    Board of Directors, 62, 63
Singletary, Don
    Home Depot, 86
Smith, Chuck
    SIFCO Forge Group, 66
Smith, Hudson
    SIFCO Forge Group, 63
Southwest Airlines, 4, 26, 28, 29, 34,
    35, 48, 49, 82, 185, 199, 203, 275
    1990-93 profits, 4
    737 philosophy, 200
    as a MicroNiche supplier, 196
    automation philosophy, 163
    charities, 91
    communicating customer service,
        128
    customer philosophy, 129
    dress code, 68
    edge, maintaining, 186
    employee recognition, 44
    MicroNiche focus, 199
    mission statement, fellow
        employees, 104
    mission/focus, 217
    Number One carrier status, 199
    Positively Outrageous Service, 110
    profit sharing, 69
    Spirit, 29, 50, 54
    superior service, 211
    ten minute turnaround, 50
    ticketless travel, 200

T

sticking close to the knitting, 165,
220
the "wow" factor, 112
time for customers, 115
timing, 15
Turbo Team responsibility, 243

U

Unleashing People Power, 19, 25, 26,
40, 62, 68, 77, 139, 201, 258, 263
crusaders, 26
defined, 17
desire to succeed, 18
different than Empowerment, 25
elimination of perks and pecking
order, 65
First Foundation, 17
goalposts, 33
information needs, 39
lesson for managers, 55
results, 25
share the vision, 34
USAir, 201

V

Value-added time
defined, 144
Varity Corp. *See* Kelsey-Hayes
VHS
competitive strategy, 211
Vision Team. *See* Turbo Team

W

Waiting time

defined, 144
Waldenbooks
bookstores, 219
Wal-Mart, 157, 186
gaining retailing's #1 spot, 218
Mexican market entry, 220
superior service, 211
Walton, Sam
Wal-Mart, 186
Wanderslaben, Mark
SIFCO Forge Group, 151
We're Doing Great, But Can Do Much
Better
Implementation strategy, 261
Welch, Jack
General Electric Corporation, 43,
89, 138, 157, 169
on change, 89
quest for efficiency/productivity,
138
Wendy's
competitive advantage, 209
Westvaco, 203
Winners
involvement with, 275
Winnik, Stan
The Home Depot, 126
Wolves at the door
implementation strategy, 235
Work-Out teams. *See* General Electric
Corporation
Wyman-Gordon
alliance with SIFCO, 7

Y

Young, Kevin
Nucor Corporation, 155

CORPORATE ORDER FORM

Here's your source for succinct information on changing the performance of any organization:

Qty	Description	Price
_____	**The Turbocharged Company; Igniting Your Business To Soar Ahead Of The Competition**—The sourcebook for companies who want to dramatically outperform their competition while providing superior returns to shareholders. Discover how 3 percent of American Businesses succeed in ways others only dream of—and what you can do to take your company to those heights.	$24.95* Hardcover
_____ Hardcover _____ Softcover	**Corporate Intensive Care; Why Businesses Fail And How To Make Them Succeed** by Larry Goddard (York-1993)—Filled with quick, effective turnaround, workout and crisis management techniques, this book is designed for companies in the downward spiral of a failing business. Learn what you can do to breathe life back into a distressed business.	$49.95* Hardcover $19.95* Softcover
_____	**Results Newsletter**—Quarterly newsletter for companies who shun the status quo and want to learn the latest techniques for dramatically enhancing business performance.	$39.95 Annual Subscription

SEND MY ORDER TO:

Name_____ Title _____

Company _____

Street address _____

_____

City _____ State _____ Zip _____

PAYMENT OPTIONS:

Order Total $ _____

❑ Mastercard/Visa # _____ expires _____

❑ Payment Enclosed   signature _____

❑ Bill Company using Purchase Order # _____

Send to: York Publishing Co.,
Chagrin Blvd. #336
Shaker Heights, OH 44120
216/491-0231 (phone)   216/491-0251 (fax)

* Please add $3.50 per book Shipping and Handling. Ohio Residents add 7% sales tax
For discounts on volume purchases, contact York Publishing Company.